LINCOLN'S
CHRISTIANITY

Also by the Author

100 Essential Lincoln Books

LINCOLN'S CHRISTIANITY

MICHAEL BURKHIMER

WESTHOLME

Yardley

Title page: The earliest known photograph of Abraham Lincoln, attributed to Nicholas H. Shepherd, taken in Springfield, Illinois, in 1846 or 1847 around the time when Lincoln had been elected to the House of Representatives. (*Library of Congress*)

Westholme Publishing, LLC
Eight Harvey Avenue
Yardley, Pennsylvania 19067
Visit our Web site at www.westholmepublishing.com

First Printing: October 2007
10 9 8 7 6 5 4 3 2 1

ISBN: 978-1-59416-053-0
(ISBN 10: 1-59416-053-8)

Printed in United States of America

For

HENRY GEORGE BURKHIMER

(1919–1996)

Veteran of the Second World War and amateur historian
who first introduced me to Lincoln on a trip to Gettysburg
and his son JOSEPH who taught me to love history

CONTENTS

INTRODUCTION

The Question of Lincoln's Faith

THIS BOOK EXPLORES ABRAHAM LINCOLN'S often nebulous relationship with the Christian religion. It is not a work of
Christian apologetics, nor is it an attempt to "prove" that Lincoln
was a freethinker. Lincoln was hardly silent on the subject of religion, yet his views are difficult to classify. He has been labeled an
infidel by some and a devout Christian by others.

Of course, there is room between these two extremes.
Founding Father John Adams prayed daily to God and was deeply
religious but did not believe the Bible was the literal word of God,
nor did he believe that Jesus was divine. Since Adams does not stir
the emotions like Lincoln, people have accepted the ambiguity and
have labeled him pious. However, with Lincoln the emotional
arguments from the two camps took hold shortly after his death
and, to some extent, continue today.[1]

I do not mean this book to be an investigation of whether
Lincoln was a good person. The legend of "Honest Abe" casts a
long shadow, and even if it does not represent the full complexity
of the man, the nickname still accurately reflects Lincoln's uncompromising morality and intolerance of hypocrisy. Rather this book
will look at what Lincoln believed and also how it may have affected the way he lived.

Lincoln's ideas about religion have been a source of contention and controversy since his death. Whether Lincoln held the Christian faith or not became a matter of importance for many in America shortly after his assassination. Because Lincoln was the nation's leader in its hour of greatest need, people thought he must have been a Godly man. The first major researched biography after his death, by Sunday school teacher Josiah Holland, argued strongly for Lincoln's basic Christian beliefs. Lincoln's third and final law partner, William Herndon, quickly responded to this argument, proclaiming that Lincoln was, at the very least, unorthodox in his beliefs. Herndon's views were expounded upon in an 1872 biography of Lincoln, ghostwritten in the name of his associate, Ward Hill Lamon. The book was a poor seller, perhaps because Americans were unable to accept that their martyred President was not an orthodox Christian.[2] Americans preferred unvarnished hagiographic accounts of Lincoln published after his death. While arguing that Lincoln was an "infidel" in his beliefs, Herndon's biography never fully justifies using that pejorative term.[3] Lincoln, tellingly, had a general skepticism of biographies of heroes. Supposedly he once said, "Biographies, as generally written, are not only misleading, but false. The author makes a wonderful hero of his subject. He magnifies his perfections, if he has any, and suppresses his imperfections. History is not history unless it is the truth."[4]

In the twentieth century, William Wolf's *The Almost Chosen People: A Study of the Religion of Abraham Lincoln* (1959) and Elton Trueblood's *Abraham Lincoln: Theologian of American Anguish* (1973) make the two clearest cases that Lincoln was a Christian, yet both works explain away too much of the evidence that runs counter to their authors' views. Since then scholars have added enormously to our understanding of Lincoln's religious beliefs, yet a consensus is lacking. A 2005 survey of the conflicting opinions declared that there was "wide disagreement concerning the exact nature of the spiritual life of our sixteenth president."[5] I believe that Lincoln's own writings, both personal and public, and recollections of those who knew him, can bring us closer to understanding how he viewed religion and what meaning it held for him.

The nature of Lincoln's Christianity has great relevance and importance today. There has been a growing prominence of religion in politics in recent decades, and the debate over what role faith should play in government and over what it means to be a Christian have continued to be core issues in the American political process. Because Lincoln is so much admired by persons of all persuasions, a study of his views on faith and spirituality can be profitable, both as a lesson in understanding and as a guide to just how much the electorate and candidates should rely on religion as a guide to good government. America could do a lot worse than follow Lincoln's example. But as this book will show, in today's political climate he probably would not be elected.

Trying to prove whether Lincoln was a Christian confronts the essential question of what it means to be a Christian. Writers have assumed there is universal agreement on what Christianity is. This simply isn't the case.

The standard most often used with Lincoln is whether he held three essential beliefs associated with the orthodox Christianity which took its final form in the fourth century A.D. at the Nicene Council: that Jesus Christ was divine and part of a Trinity, that Christ died for the sins of the world, and that faith in this doctrine is necessary for one to gain salvation. This is a gross simplification of the complexity of Christian belief, but it is a foundation almost all are familiar with. How Lincoln approached these tenets will be discussed in this book.

Inevitably, there are quandaries that each reader may have to answer for themselves about what makes a "true" Christian. Does belief itself make one a Christian, or can actions by themselves be enough to qualify someone as being a Christian? Christ himself said, "Ye shall know them by their fruits. Do men gather grapes of thorns, or figs of thistles?" (Matthew 7:16).

The best sources for examining Lincoln's religion are his own words and those of his contemporaries. Yet this is not always a sure path, because as a prominent citizen and later as President, Lincoln may have found it politically expedient to use biblical language or religious sentiments. This was so much part of the discourse of nineteenth-century American that it hardly qualifies as dissembling, but it may not have always reflected Lincoln's true beliefs. Also, his contemporaries were not consistent in reporting what Lincoln told them on the subject of his faith. Therefore, not all of this testimony is equal. Many of the people who spoke about Lincoln's Christianity had agendas of their own, and after his assassination the tendency to idealize the beloved President was considerable. Care must be taken in evaluating the evidence, even from primary sources and eyewitnesses.

To truly understand Lincoln's Christianity one must go back to the beginnings of the faith. Lincoln was a Bible reader, and an avid student of the Gospels. Time and time again he turned to them for wisdom and quotations to deal with the problems he faced. He tended to skip over later glosses in the Gospel story and go to the heart of what Christ actually taught. Notably, Lincoln did not quote from the Gospel of John, which is a later and more spiritual presentation of Jesus. Lincoln's manner of speaking was logical and straightforward, perhaps better suited to the teachings of Jesus from the earlier sources that appear in the Gospels of Mark, Matthew, and Luke.

A final point should be made about Lincoln's time. Lincoln was born in the early nineteenth century, by which time whatever religious skepticism that was in vogue in the Enlightenment and through the late eighteenth century was fading away from the American cultural scene. Revivalism was taking hold across the country, in particular on the frontier where Lincoln spent his youth. During his early life Lincoln would have been more at home in terms of religion with the generation before him (although his parents were devout Baptists). It should be remembered that Lincoln's early religious beliefs were shaped in this often emotional environment.[6]

That is not to say that Lincoln was alone in his distance from orthodox Christian doctrine. There were Unitarians and others who questioned key beliefs of the majority, yet they were in a very distinct minority, and Lincoln's early years were not spent in their company.

THE LINCOLN SCHOLAR DAVID HERBERT DONALD once spoke of people trying to "get right by Lincoln." On the subject of religion, people are instead trying to get Lincoln right by them. The desire to attribute to Lincoln one's own religious views can be overwhelming for some. I hope I have escaped that pitfall, but as Lincoln once said, people should "show their hands."[7] I should disclose that I am an unabashed admirer of the sixteenth president, and I have always felt, as his secretary John Hay observed, "Lincoln with all his foibles is the greatest character since Christ."[8] I will also confess to a liberal Roman Catholic faith—a skeptical and questioning faith, but a faith nonetheless. I hope those who judge this book will not hold these beliefs against me.

Much of the material quoted in this book by Lincoln's contemporaries is from interviews taken quickly or from people who were not always careful in their spelling. I have let their words stand as written. Also, the Bible that Lincoln read as an adult was the King James Version, and thus all references in this book are to it.[9]

Chapter 1

FRONTIER RELIGION

There was absolutely nothing to excite ambition for education.
—*Abraham Lincoln to Jesse Fell, December 20, 1859*

JOSHUA SPEED TURNED THE KNOB and entered Abraham Lincoln's bedroom. He had come to visit the president at a cottage on the grounds of the Soldiers' Home in Washington, where Lincoln often escaped the White House for more pleasant conditions during the summers. Near nightfall, Speed found Lincoln, one of his closest friends and a former confidant, reading intently by the window. The book was none other than the Bible. Many years before, Speed's family had given Lincoln a Bible as a gift, but the Lincoln whom Speed had known almost thirty years was not one who had found solace in the Christian religion and its holy text. Speed remarked, "I am glad to see you so profitably engaged." Lincoln replied, "Yes, I am profitably engaged." "Well," said Speed, "if you have recovered from your skepticism, I am sorry to say that I have not." Lincoln placed his hand on Speed's shoulder and replied, "You are wrong Speed, take all of this book upon reason that you can, and the balance on faith and you will live and die a happier and better man."[1]

This exchange took place in the summer of 1864, when Lincoln was at a low ebb in his presidency. The coming election would be a referendum on both his ability to win the war and his decision to emancipate the slaves. Ulysses S. Grant and George Meade were stalled before Petersburg and Richmond while William T. Sherman seemed to be frustrated in front of Atlanta. Lincoln's prospects looked dim. His wife recalled that he read the Bible "a good deal about 1864."[2]

There can be no doubt about Speed's implication that Lincoln had a youthful religious skepticism. The evidence on this point is almost unarguable. Lincoln's own words, and those of his contemporaries, clearly attest to it. For the first forty years of his life, Lincoln refused to accept the Christian religion that permeated the world around him.

This skepticism was not simply another idiosyncrasy of Lincoln's personality. Lincoln's early life and the nature of the surrounding religious environment contributed to it. To understand Lincoln's somewhat ambiguous attitude toward the Christian religion one must take into account the experiences of his youth.

Lincoln's parents, Thomas and Nancy, were members of the Little Mount Baptist Church in Kentucky when Abraham was born in 1809. When the family removed to Indiana in 1816, Thomas joined the Pigeon Creek Baptist Church. Of the many shades of Baptists of the day, the Lincolns belonged to what would be called Separate Baptists. The difference between the Separate and the Regular Baptists came down to acceptance of a creed. The Regulars accepted what was called the "Philadelphia Confession of Faith," which was an orthodox Christian creed.[3]

The Separatists, "sometimes called hard-shells," refused to adopt "any creed but the Bible." The Separatists were generally more extreme in their view of predestination, the idea that God had "elected" those whom he was to save. The notion of freewill did not really exist for them. "Other characteristic features were foot washing, rejection of paid and educated ministry, and opposition to musical instruments in worship. There was also among 'hard shells' resistance to missionary activity in foreign lands, and to such newfangled notions as Sunday schools for unregenerate children."[4] An early biography of Lincoln relates, "The family was imbued with a peculiar, intense, but unenlightened form of Christianity, mingled with curious superstition, prevalent in the backwoods, and begotten by the influence of the vast wilderness upon illiterate men of a rude native force." Even many years after he left home, the reading of certain Bible verses conjured up in Lincoln's mind the tones of his mother's voice repeating them as she went about her household chores. This may have been his happiest memory of his mother.[5]

A taste of the religious atmosphere can be seen in William Herndon's description of a camp meeting in 1816. Herndon, who was Lincoln's law partner and early biographer, collected a great deal of information about Lincoln's youth shortly after his death. In the following account he mistook an unnamed couple to be Lincoln's parents. According to the story, a young man and woman went through the ritual of marriage and its climax in a rather loud and boisterous ceremony. It ends as "Slowly and gracefully they worked their way towards the centre, singing, shouting, hugging, and kissing, generally their own sex, until at last nearer and nearer they came. The centre of the altar was reached, and the two closed, with their arms around each other, the man singing and shouting at the top of his voice, 'I have Jesus in my arms, Sweet as honey, strong as bacon ham.'" Herndon once said, "The great predominating elements of Mr. Lincoln's peculiar character were: first, his great capacity and power of reason." It is not hard to imagine Lincoln looking back with a shudder at some of these scenes. William Barton, a minister and Lincoln historian, recounts traveling among the people of Lincoln's early manhood. "In the mind of most if not all of the Baptist preachers whom Lincoln heard while he was at New Salem, a belief that the earth was round was sufficient to brand a man as an infidel."[6]

Life on the frontier shaped its religious character. Barton observed, "A religion less gentle or more refined would not have served so well the rude conditions of the frontier." The harsh conditions the settlers lived through, and the sudden deaths that often overtook their family members could be understood within the framework of predestination. A baby's death was part of God's plan. Human beings were not capable of understanding the workings of God, so those tragedies could be looked at as part of a larger plan. Also, those who felt they were the "elect" of God could look forward to meeting their family members again in heaven. One historian writes, "The Pigeon Creek Church, for example, established as part of its articles of faith that 'we believe in one god the father, the word & holly gost who haith created all things that are created by the word of his power for his pleasure' and that 'we believe in Election by grace given us in Christ Jesus Before the world began & that God Cawls, generates and sanctifies all who are made meat [meet] for Glory by his special grace.'" Since Lincoln's father was one of the most important men in the Indiana church, it is hard to disagree with the historian's assertion that "Abraham Lincoln's life in Indiana was lived in an atmosphere of what William Barton called 'a Calvinism that would have out-Calvined Calvin.'" This sense of being the "elect" was vital for many in Lincoln's early surroundings, as a means of comfort since death could strike anyone at any time. Death was so common that someone once remembered that Thomas Lincoln, a carpenter and farmer, "was always making a coffin for someone." It helped to believe that the time of one's death was part of God's mysterious plan.[7]

There can be little doubt that both of Lincoln's parents were utterly sincere in their beliefs. Both turned to their Christian faith at death for comfort. As she lay dying from what was called the "milk sickness," a sickness gained by drinking the milk of cows that had eaten a poisonous root, at the age of thirty-five, Nancy Hanks Lincoln called nine-year-old Abraham to her side. She put her hand on his head and told him to be "kind and good to his father and sister." She then expressed a hope that they might live, "as they had been taught by her, to love their kindred and worship God." When Thomas Lincoln was on what he thought was his deathbed in 1849, he had his stepson, John Johnston, write Lincoln and say that though he never had met Lincoln's wife Mary Todd Lincoln, "he wonts me to tell your wife that he Loves hure & want hur to prepare to meet him at ower Savours feet." Lincoln rushed to Coles County to see his father, but it was a false alarm. Two years later when his father was on his real deathbed, Johnston again, but unsuccessfully, wrote Lincoln to come. In an almost pathetic scene, Johnston said that the lonely Thomas Lincoln was sure that God "has a Crown of glory, prepared for *him*."[8]

Despite their strong faith, Lincoln showed irreverence toward his parents' religion early in life. The first extant writing from his childhood sum book includes this bit of doggerel:

> Abraham Lincoln
> his hand and pen
> he will be good but
> god knows When

Many have looked at this as a sign of Lincoln's piety, though it seems far too flippant for that. As Barton writes, "If one were to make a creed out of any of his poetry in this period, it were better to find it in his jingle, about the Kickapoo Indian, Johnny

Kongapod. He was supposed to have composed an epitaph for himself:

> Here lies poor Johnny Kongapod;
> Have mercy on him, gracious God,
> As he would do if he was God
> And you were Johnny Kongapod."[9]

Lincoln's other early poetry is sad and pessimistic. He wrote the following old Calvinist verses beside some math problems in his sum book:

> . . . Time What an emty vaper
> tis and days how swift they are swift as an indian
> arr[row]
> fly on like shooting star the present moment Just [is
> here]
> then slides away in h[as]te that we [can] never say
> they['re ours]
> but [only say] th[ey]'re past

The sentiments in this poem, untouched with a whiff of redemption or grace, would be downright blasphemous to many in Lincoln's early environment. The verses also foreshadow what would be Lincoln's lifelong passion for poetry with a melancholy theme.[10]

Lincoln's father had helped to build the Pigeon Creek Baptist Church in 1821. When he became a trustee two years later Thomas Lincoln recommended his fourteen-year-old son as sexton. This required Lincoln to keep the church clean, provide firewood for the cold winters, and keep candles in supply. Despite these responsibilities, Lincoln made light of the church services he attended. Lincoln's stepsister remembers, "Abe would go out to work in the field—get up on a stump and repeat almost word for word the sermon he had heard the Sunday before—Call the Children and friends around him—His father would come and make him quit—send him to work." One scholar explains, "He would not only recall the sermons word for word, but would also give some emphasis to the preacher's eccentricities both of mannerism and voice." As far as Lincoln ever thought of actually joining the church at which he was sexton, Ida Tarbell tells us, "Abraham Lincoln never joined Pigeon Church. Its peculiar ceremonies made little or no impression upon him." When the twenty-one-year-old Lincoln left Indiana with his family for Illinois, he was not a member of the church.[11]

It may well be that Lincoln's youthful refusal of his parents' faith was part of a larger rejection of his father and his world. Thomas Lincoln seemed to favor his stepson John, who stayed with him after Lincoln left to make his own way. Thomas was also at times physically abusive toward his son. He would "knock him a rod" for perceived impudence or "slash him" for neglecting his work to read. Lincoln concluded that this was poor parenting, and he rejected corporal punishment for his own children and indulged their rowdiness. Lincoln's life followed a completely different trajectory than his father's. Lincoln described Indiana in his early years as a place where "there was absolutely nothing to excite ambition of education." In his mind, the religious thought of this same place was similarly uninspiring.[12]

As a young man Lincoln could be disdainful of clergymen and church services, as his impersonation of ministers shows. In an 1834 article that went out under a different man's name, Lincoln also attacked his political opponent Peter Cartwright, a circuit-riding preacher: "I believe the people in this country are in some degree priest ridden." He continued, speaking of Cartwright personally, "He has one of the largest and best improved farms in Sangamon county, with other property in proportion. And how has he got it? Only by the contributions he has been able to levy upon and collect from a priest ridden church." Cartwright was also "a most abandoned hypocrite." When he later ran against Cartwright for Congress in 1846, Lincoln supposedly visited a revival service Cartwright was holding. As Ida Tarbell tells it, "When Cartwright was urging sinners to come to the mourners' bench he often appealed by name to persons in his audience, and this night, seeing Mr. Lincoln, he began to urge him forward, finally shouting: 'If you are not going to repent and go to Heaven, Mr. Lincoln, where are you going?' Lincoln slowly rose to his feet. 'I am going to Congress, Brother Cartwright.'" We do not know whether this story is apocryphal, but the fact that people repeated it says something for Lincoln's reputation for irreverence.[13]

One of Lincoln's favorite jokes was about an unfortunate preacher, dressed in fine clothes, who began to preach one day. He started with the text, "I am the Christ whom I shall represent today." Unfortunately, as he began, a lizard or scorpion began to run up his leg. As Lincoln told it, "the old man began to slap away on his legs, but missed the Lizard, and kept getting higher up, he unbuttoned his pants at one snatch, and kicked off his pants, but the thing kept on up his back; the next motion was for the collar button of his shirt, and off it went. In the house was an old Lady, who took a good look at him, and said, well, if you represent Christ, I am done believing in the Bible."[14]

Lincoln also was fond of telling a story about a poor minister who couldn't get money from his flock. Lincoln related, "He at last told the non-paying trustees that he must have his money, as he was suffering for the necessities of life. 'Money!' replied the trustees, 'you preach for money? We thought you preached for the good of souls!' 'Souls!' responded the reverend, 'I can't eat souls; and if I could it would take a thousand such as yours to make a meal!'" Lincoln even joked when he moved to Springfield in

1837, "I've never been to church yet, nor probably shall not be soon. I stay away because I am conscious I should not know how to behave myself."[15]

Tellingly, no one who was close to him seems to recall Lincoln making a confession of faith of the Christian religion. Arguments from silence are hardly the best, still the broad range of people who could not remember Lincoln doing so is notable. Lincoln could have been quiet about his beliefs, but it is likely that there would have been some indication of them.

One of Lincoln's few close friends of many years was Illinois Senator Orville Hickman Browning. Asked after Lincoln's death about the president's beliefs, he replied, "Of his religious opinions I am not able to speak. It is more than probable we have conversed upon religious subjects; but, if we did, I am not able to call back to my recollection anything which was said in such conversations, with such distinctness as to warrant me repeating it." Three years later, Browning said, "I can't recollect any occasion on which we ever had any talk about the Christian religion."[16]

Josiah and Elizabeth Crawford were neighbors of Lincoln in Indiana, and both Lincoln and his father had worked for Josiah Crawford. When Elizabeth Crawford was asked by Herndon about Lincoln's religious beliefs she answered, "you wished me to tell you whether Abraham lincoln ever made Any pretensions of religeon during his Stay in this country. . . . I never heard of his ever making any such pretensions. . . . I dont think he ever did though he Seemed to be A well wisher."[17]

Lincoln's mother's cousin Dennis Hanks recalled about Lincoln's religion, "I Cant tell But I Dont Think he held any Views Very Strong." A year after Lincoln's death his stepmother said, "Abe read the bible some, though not as much as said: he sought more congenial books. . . . Abe had no particular religion—didn't think of that question at that time, if he ever did—He never talked about it." Still, she did not doubt Lincoln was welcomed by God after his death. "Abe & his father are in Heaven I have no doubt, and I want to go there—go where they are—God bless Ab[raha]m."[18]

Lincoln could mine the Bible for humor. Probably the best remembered of Lincoln's pranks was his writing of a parody of the scriptures called "The Chronicles of Rueben." Although no copy of the chronicle has been found in Lincoln's hand, it was recalled in detail by a number of persons who read it at the time, and several wrote down what they remembered. Written in a pseudo-biblical style, Lincoln's account chastised Rueben and Charles Grigsby for the death of his sister Sarah in childbirth. Sarah was married to another Grigsby brother, and Lincoln thought the family had treated her poorly and did not do enough to save her life. Furthermore, when the two brothers were married in 1829 Lincoln was snubbed and not invited to the weddings. To get even, Lincoln arranged with an accomplice to switch the beds of the two grooms so that they would be led to the wrong wives that night. The Chronicles recount this episode. Written like the Old Testament, they begin: "Now there was man whose name was Reuben, and the same was very great in substance; in horses and cattle and swine, and a very great household. It came to pass when the sons of Reuben grew up that they were desirous of taking themselves wives, and being too well known as to honor in their own country they took a journey into a far country and there procured for themselves wives."

The Chronicles also told the story of an imaginary same-sex marriage of another Grigsby brother Billy:

> . . . he is married to Natty.
> So Billy and Natty agreed very well;
> And mamma's well pleased at the match.[19]

Lincoln could also use God as part of a joke on the stump. Once when running for reelection for the Illinois legislature, in the mid-1830s, he faced a man who switched parties and was given a plum job for doing so. The man had then built a fine house and had a lightning rod installed. He attacked Lincoln using the usual rough-and-tumble style so prevalent on the frontier. Lincoln waited his turn and then let loose, "I would rather die now, than, like the gentleman, change my politics, and simultaneous with the change receive an office worth $3,000 per year, and then have to erect a lightning-rod over my house to protect a guilty conscience from an offended God." He also made light of the idea of rewards in the hereafter in an 1842 speech on temperance, by inserting an old joke. He told the crowd, "Still, in addition to this, there is something so ludicrous in *promises* of good, or *threats* of evil, a great way off, as to render the whole subject with which they are connected, easily turned into ridicule. 'Better lay down that spade you're stealing, Paddy,—if you don't you'll pay for it at the day of judgment.' 'By the powers, if ye'll credit me so long, I'll take another, jist.'"[20]

It is not as if the Christianity of his parents had no effect on Lincoln. The doctrine of predestination remained part of his philosophy for the rest of his life. In fact, he often repeated the famous lines of Hamlet: "There's a divinity that shapes our ends, Rough-hew them how we will."

Lincoln scholar Wayne Temple writes of a "predestination which permeated his very being. This belief became much more prominent when his national responsibilities as President of the United States became very heavy upon his shoulders." Mary Todd Lincoln said of her husband, "Mr Lincolns maxim and philosophy was—'What is to be will be and no cares of ours can arrest the decree.'" Political associate Joseph Gillespie remembered, "Mr Lincoln told me once that he could not avoid believing in predestination." Herndon agreed with this assessment and called it "Mr.

Lincoln's fatalism," though Herndon thought of it more as a philosophical position than a theological one. He remembered, "First, he believed that both matter and mind are governed by certain irrefragable and irresistible laws, and that no prayers of ours could arrest their operation in the least . . . the laws of human nature are persistent and permanent and could not be reversed. . . . He said, while he was President, that he did not rule events, during any time in his administration, but that events ruled him." Herndon may overstate the case for effect, but his general view is correct.[21]

David Herbert Donald has perceptively seen the importance of this fatalism in understanding Lincoln's personality and his ambition. Donald writes, "From Lincoln's fatalism derived some of his most lovable traits: his compassion, his tolerance, his willingness to overlook mistakes. That belief did not, of course, lead him to lethargy or dissipation. Like thousands of Calvinists who believed in predestination, he worked indefatigably for a better world—for himself, for his family, and for his nation." One of the reasons Lincoln could be generous and not personally vindictive toward the South is that he saw them as caught up in forces beyond their control or acting out the will of Providence. As he once said of the South, "They are just what we would be in their situation." This facet of Lincoln's philosophy would be given clear expression to in his Second Inaugural Address (see Chapter 6).[22]

THE CALVINIST VIEW OF THE WORLD was Lincoln's by birthright. The first Lincoln in America was Samuel Lincoln, who arrived in the Massachusetts Bay Colony with his brothers in 1637. Like thousands of others who fled England during the Great Migration, they left for a variety of reasons. Samuel was a weaver, could not find work, and had been persecuted for his Puritan beliefs. His sect believed that the Church of England was suspect and not true to the real Christian faith. Like other Calvinists, they believed that God had chosen them as the "elect" and that they were living out a plan God had made for them. Their task was to create a "City upon a Hill" for the world to study and emulate. This was not an easy or assured task because, as one student of Puritanism has pointed out, "Their success as a model Christian community was by no means inevitable, since it depended upon an unwavering fidelity to their divine calling." As further generations of Lincolns moved south they abandoned the Puritan religion, but its world-view followed Lincoln into Kentucky.[23]

Ultimately the Puritan worldview is full of contradictions. One student of the early Massachusetts Puritans praised it for all it had done for America but also commented on its dark effects on the minds of its followers. He wrote, "Puritanism required that he rest his whole hope in Christ but taught him that Christ would ulti-mately reject him unless before he was born God had foreordained his salvation. Puritanism required that man refrain from sin but told him he would sin anyhow. Puritanism required that he reform the world in the image of God's holy kingdom but taught him that the evil of the world was incurable and inevitable." Lincoln would reject the notion of the "elect." In fact, he shared the Scottish poet Robert Burns's disdainful view on the matter, as will be seen later. However, he still believed in much of the Puritan worldview regarding the absence of free will.[24]

Instead of predestination, Lincoln turned his Calvinism into what he called "the Doctrine of Necessity." Herndon described it this way: "Things were to be, and they came, irresistibly came, doomed to come . . . the fates settled things as by the doom of the powers, and laws, universal, absolute, and eternal, ruled the uni-verse of matter and mind. . . . [Man] is simply a *simple tool*, a mere cog in the wheel, a part, a small part, of this vast iron machine, that strikes and cuts, grinds and mashes, all things, including man, that resist it."[25]

It is possible that Herndon, in his desire to rebut the pious biographers that were so abundant after Lincoln's death, was overly dramatic in his comments about Lincoln's thinking. As Herndon's own biographer states, "But so anxious was Herndon to prevent his partner's becoming a Calvinist demigod that he overstated his case." Herndon himself was unorthodox in his beliefs. He once wrote, "I believe that the Bible is the revelation of God, and that Jesus was the son of God, and so do I believe that the Declaration of Independence is the revelation of God and George Washington, a son of God." However, much of what Herndon said and wrote matches up with Lincoln's own words about necessity. If perhaps engaging in too many flourishes, Herndon was correct in his analysis.[26]

Lincoln felt that humans acted most on motives that were as set and as immutable as natural law. Here was Calvinism without the election. Instead of viewing oneself as greater than others because God had chosen one for salvation and others for damnation, Lincoln thought that humans should be humble because they were acting out what nature and God had set for them.[27]

This humble and nonjudgmental point of view appealed to the greatest American freethinker of the nineteenth century, Robert Ingersoll. Ingersoll focused on the evidence of Lincoln's early life to paint his picture of Lincoln's religious views. Years after Lincoln's death, Ingersoll wrote, "He was a logician. Logic is the necessary product of intelligence and sincerity. It cannot be learned. It is the child of a clear head and good heart. He was candid, and with candor often deceived the deceitful. He had an intellect without arrogance, genius without pride, and religion without cant—that is to say, without bigotry and without deceit."[28]

Others shared Lincoln's views as the Great Awakening of religious revival swept the nation in the early nineteenth century. Many scenes like Lincoln's parents' religious experience were played out across the frontier. Lincoln on the other hand had more in common with the Unitarians of New England at the time. One historian observes, "While the cool Unitarian of Boston shrank form the camp-meeting spirit, he agreed with the evangelicals that man and his life on earth are good, or at least may become so. . . . The most extreme form of the old idea, the Calvinist doctrine of total depravity, gave way to extreme forms of faith in progress." Many felt that they were called upon by God through predestination to try to improve the world, and a great increase in reform movements like abolitionism, women's rights, and prohibition flourished during Lincoln's youth. Of course, many put greater emphasis on predestination as being divine, instead of Lincoln's more naturalistic view.[29]

Another aspect of his parents' religion that Lincoln adopted was the study of the Bible. One of his Indiana neighbors said, "i cannot tel you what his notions of the bible he was a great talker on the scriptures and read it a great deal." Lincoln's stepmother and cousin both admit that he sometimes read the Bible, although he may have not believed it was the divinely inspired word of God. In his first ever campaign for the Illinois Legislature in 1832, Lincoln stressed the need for public education because it was important for people to be able to read about the history of their country and appreciate its freedoms. He also saw "the advantages and satisfaction to be derived from all being able to read the scriptures and other works, both of a religious and moral nature, for themselves." It is intriguing that Lincoln mentions "other works" in the same breath as "the scriptures," suggesting he placed other books on moral wisdom on the same plane as the Bible.[30]

Some of the most revealing letters Lincoln ever wrote were to his most intimate friend, Joshua Speed. Speed could rightly say, "He disclosed his whole heart to me." For four years they lived together and even shared the same bed. Both got "cold feet" before their weddings and acted as counselors for each other. In their exchanges of letters Lincoln touches on predestination, and in letters to Speed's half-sister, he mentions the Bible. This evidence is valuable because it is from private letters between two close friends.[31]

Speed was engaged to Fanny Henning in the latter part of 1841. He worried if he truly loved his fiancée and thought marriage might be a mistake. Lincoln consistently told him that his worries were groundless. In a way Lincoln was reassuring himself, because his own engagement to Mary Todd had been broken off in late 1840, and he wanted Speed to be happy, as a sign that he too could be happy in matrimony. When Speed was married in February 1842, he found marriage to be much more congenial than he had thought possible. Lincoln was ecstatic. He viewed the whole matter as another example of predestination: "I believe God made me one of the instruments of bringing your Fanny and you together, which union, I have no doubt He had fore-ordained. Whatever he designs, he will do for me yet. 'Stand *still* and see the salvation of the Lord is my text just now.'"[32]

Lincoln also had a good word about the Bible with Speed's half-sister Mary. When he visited Speed in Kentucky in 1841, he formed an affectionate friendship with her and jokingly referred to themselves as "something of cronies." While he was in Kentucky, Speed's mother had given him a Bible as a present. Lincoln wrote Mary, "Tell your mother that I have not got her 'present' with me; but I intend to read it regularly when I return home. I doubt not that it is really, as she says, the best cure for the 'Blues' could one take it according to the truth." The qualification at the end of the statement confirms Lincoln's skepticism during this period of his life, yet it also shows someone who was not averse to reading scripture "regularly."[33]

FOLLOWING IN THE FOOTSTEPS OF THE great skeptic Thomas Paine, Lincoln saw Jesus Christ as a man of wisdom. Paine, who was certainly not a Christian when he wrote *The Age of Reason*, his most famous works on religion, wrote: "Nothing that is here said can apply even with the most disrespect to, the real character of Jesus Christ. He was a virtuous and amiable man. The morality that he preached and practiced was of the most benevolent kind; and though similar systems of morality had been preached by Confucius, and by some of the Greek philosophers, many years before; by Quakers since; and by many good men in all ages, it has not been exceeded by any."

Similarly, in an 1843 political circular Lincoln said, "That 'union is strength' is a truth that has been known, illustrated and declared, in various ways and forms in all ages of the world. That great fabulist and philosopher, Aesop, illustrated it by his fable of the bundle of sticks; and he whose wisdom surpasses that of all philosophers, has declared that a 'house divided against itself cannot stand.'" Of course this quotation, which is found in all three Synoptic Gospels, would be used again by Lincoln in 1858 when attacking Stephen Douglas's stance on slavery. Here, however, it is just an exhortation for unity within his political party as part of its electoral strategy. As Lincoln put the Bible on the same level as other "moral works," he here sees Jesus Christ chiefly as a philosopher. Jesus' wisdom is greater than other philosophers; however, he is not the savior or son of God.[34]

Lincoln maintained this respectful distance from Jesus throughout his life. Although he had known hardship and the death of his mother early in life, he emerged from his parents' shelter with his own ideas and reservations about religion intact. Life on his own would allow him to test and explore his beliefs further.

Chapter 2

THE YOUNG SKEPTIC

It is true that in early life I was inclined to believe in what I understand
is called the "Doctrine of necessity."
—*Abraham Lincoln, "Handbill Replying to Charges of Infidelity"*

L INCOLN'S SKEPTICISM WAS STRONG in Indiana, but it flourished when he left his parents' home in 1831 after moving to
Illinois. When he was nineteen Lincoln had taken a flatboat to
New Orleans with a friend to sell its cargo. Now he decided to
take a second flatboat journey to New Orleans, this time with
John Hanks and his stepbrother. His flatboat had gotten caught on
the dam built for the mill of a little Illinois village called New
Salem on the Sangamon River. Lincoln managed to free his flatboat by boring a hole in it and letting the water run out until it
righted itself. This so impressed Denton Offutt, the man behind
the New Orleans venture, that he vowed to build a store in New
Salem and have Lincoln run it when he made his way back. After
the trip Lincoln didn't have any better prospects, so he settled in
the village.[1]

New Salem can rightfully be called Lincoln's "alma mater."
The years he lived there, from 1831 to 1837, were some of the most
extraordinary of his life. He started out poor with ragged clothes and

appearance, but was a transformed man when he left. In New Salem he entered politics, studied law, served in the military, and set the course for his life. Despite the stereotype of a frontier settlement, New Salem was hardly an intellectual wasteland. One study of the village recounts how Lincoln passed some of his time. "Lincoln has spent his leisure from the duties of keeping store in perfecting his education and in the study of Shakespeare, [Robert] Burns, and the current fiction of the day, and he loved to go fishing with Jack Kelso, one of those peculiar, impractical geniuses—well educated, a lover of nature, with the soul of a poet and all of a poet's impracticability, and who could 'recite Shakespeare and Burns by the hour.'" There was also a debating society that met twice monthly, and Lincoln spoke there frequently.[2]

Compared to what he could get his hands on in Indiana, a wealth of books were available to Lincoln in New Salem. According to one resident, "History and poetry & the newspapers constituted the most of his reading. . . . Burns seemed to be his favorite. . . . Used to sit up late of nights reading, & would recommence in the morning when he got up." Lincoln read Gibbon's *Decline and Fall of the Roman Empire*, in which much of the fall of Rome was blamed on Christianity. He also read Rollin's *Ancient History*. A schoolteacher in the village remembered, "In New Salem he devoted more time to reading the scripture, books on science and comments on law and to the acquisition of Knowledge of men & things than any man I ever knew and it has been my task to teach in the primary school Forty five years." He also thought that Lincoln was the "most studious, diligent strait forward young man in the pursuit of a knowledge of literature than any among the five thousand I have taught in scho[ol]."[3]

In New Salem Lincoln read the works of some eighteenth-century skeptics, such as Thomas Paine and Constantin de Volney's *Ruins of Civilization*. Paine's *The Age of Reason*, a defense of

Deism and an attack on the idea of revealed religion, enumerates many of the supposed logical and moral defects of the Bible. Volney too was critical of the accuracy of the Bible and said that morality was the only part of religion that one could see and prove. His book opens with, "Hail, solitary ruins, holy sepulchers and silent walls! you I invoke; to you I address my prayer. . . . Oh Ruins! To your school I will return! I will seek again the calm of your solitudes; and there far from the afflicting spectacle of passion, I will cherish . . . the love of man . . . and build my own happiness on the promotion of his." Volney put man in front of God, and he had no patience with the idea that civilizations fell due to the wrath of God. Lincoln would bring these arguments out in debate with his fellow citizens. He shocked local townswoman Parthena Hill with his answer to her question, "Do you really believe there isn't any future state?" Lincoln replied, "Mrs. Hill, I'm afraid there isn't. It isn't a pleasant thing to think that when we die that is the last of us." Lincoln's unorthodoxy was shocking to many of the pious of New Salem, but it was not unique to him among its citizens.[4]

These new views led Lincoln to write a book in 1834-1835. This was remembered by many of the villagers and has come down to us as his "Infidelity," which was not a printed book rather written on several pages of foolscap. The title derives from the common use of "infidel" for an unbeliever, rather than the modern sense of unfaithfulness. It is not extant; in most versions of the story it is consigned to the flames by Parthena Hill's husband Samuel in order to save Lincoln's future political career.[5]

The earliest public account of this document came in an Illinois Democratic paper while Lincoln was President in 1862. The *Menard Axis* asked the son of Samuel and Parthena Hill, John, to write a short description of Lincoln in his early years in New Salem. Hill most likely got the information from his parents. The article, called "A Romance of Reality," is a spoof contrasting

Lincoln's years at New Salem with the station of the Presidency
that he occupied in 1862. The article makes light of his love affair
with Ann Rutledge and his poor attire in his New Salem years. Of
Lincoln's "Infidelity" he states, "he employed his intellectual fac-
ulties in writing a dissertation against the doctrine of the divinity of
the scriptures. Of this he soon repented, and consigned his produc-
tion to the flames." John Hill probably thought that the idea of an
infidel President would not play well with the voters in rural
Illinois.[6]

Some have argued that this "book" wasn't really a a defense of
"infidel" beliefs, but Lincoln's more liberal and universal version
of Christianity. The local schoolteacher, Mentor Graham, claimed
that Lincoln had showed him his writing, and that it was a defense
of universal salvation—a position Lincoln adopted later in life.
However, because he told Parthena Hill that there was no "future
state," the notion that the document included a notion of universal
salvation is very unlikely. There was probably something about
how eternal punishment was not logical, but there are too many
other witnesses to the other arguments to call it Christian.[7]

For example, another resident remembered that, "I do know
that Mr Lincoln did write a letter, pamphlet—book or what not
on the faith as I understand he held—denying Special & miraculous Revelation—Inspiration & Conception—As I stated Lincoln
thought that God predestined things—and governed the universe
by Law—nothing going by accident. . . . His mind was full of terrible Enquiry—and was skeptical in a good sense." Herndon himself recalled, "The points that Mr. Lincoln tried to demonstrate
(in his book) were: First, That the Bible was not God's revelation;
and, Second, That Jesus was not the Son of God. *I assert this on
my own knowledge, and on my veracity.*" If one wanted to argue
against Lincoln's criticism of orthodox Christianity in the book

and in general, they would have a high hurdle to clear against all the evidence.[8]

Lincoln's skeptical discussions and arguments became known to many through gossip, and they were controversial enough to affect his early political career. Lincoln was subscribed to the Whig philosophy, which advocated the betterment of the country both morally and economically through government action. Lincoln believed fervently that economic improvements to the frontier such as banks, roads, canals, and railroads would help change the deprivation that he and others had experienced. The Democrats, in contrast, thought that any attempt to do this would benefit the rich at the expense of the common man.[9] Lincoln first ran for the Illinois Legislature in 1832, and was defeated mostly due to his newness in the area. After being elected in 1834, he was reelected three times and served until 1842. His ability was recognized early, and he even served as Whig floor leader for a time.

When Lincoln was the Whig candidate for the Seventh Congressional District of Illinois in 1846, his Democratic opponent was none other than the Methodist preacher Peter Cartwright, whom Lincoln had skewered in the ghostwritten letter years before. The Seventh District was the one Whig stronghold in the state. Cartwright's campaign could not get much traction on the traditional Democratic issues, so he stooped to playing the religion card. As a popular and effective circuit-riding preacher, Cartwright was in a unique position; nobody would be more authoritative when it came to the subject of Christian orthodoxy. Toward the end of the campaign, he charged that Lincoln was an infidel. One observer remembered that "Cartwright *sneaked* through this part of the district after Lincoln, and grossly misrepresented him."[10]

Lincoln so feared this tactic that he wrote a handbill answering Cartwright, although some of his friends never felt the need to issue it. It did go out in parts of the district. In the handbill he never mentions Cartwright by name, keeping the denial more general. It is an important document, however, because it is in Lincoln's own hand and touches on so many of the religious themes that he thought about in the first forty years of his life. It reads in full:

> To The Voters of the Seventh Congressional District Fellow Citizens:
>
> A charge having got into circulation in some of the neighborhoods of this District, in substance that I am an open scoffer at Christianity, I have by the advice of some friends concluded to notice the subject in this form. That I am not a member of any Christian Church, is true; but I have never denied the truth of the Scripture; and I have never spoken with intentional disrespect of religion in general, or of any denomination of Christians in particular. It is true that in early life I was inclined to believe in what I understand is called the "Doctrine of necessity" — that is, that the human mind is impelled to action, or held in rest by some power, over which the mind itself has no control; and I have sometimes (with one, two or three, but never publicly) tried to maintain this opinion in argument — The habit of arguing thus however, I have, entirely left off for more than five years — And I add here, I have always understood this same opinion to be held by several of the Christian denominations. The foregoing, is the whole truth, briefly stated, in relation to myself upon this subject.
>
> I do not think I could myself, be brought to support a man for office, whom I knew to be an open enemy of, and scoffer at, religion. Leaving the higher matter of

eternal consequences, between him and his maker, I still do not think any man has the right thus to insult the feelings, and injure the morals, of a community in which he may live. If, then I was guilty of such conduct, I should blame no man who would condemn me for it; but I do blame those, whoever they may be, who falsely put such a charge in circulation against me.[11]

Here Lincoln is most explicit about the "Doctrine of necessity." He states that the mind is "impelled to action" or "held in rest" by a power over which the mind has no control. He does not hint anywhere that the "power" is God; here again is Calvinism without the Deity. Free will is absent if the mind is in the power of some other force, which Lincoln calls "necessity." Note in this handbill Lincoln's own words back up what others said about his views on "fatalism." Lincoln also acknowledges that he occasionally argued these points with a few friends but "never publicly." Lincoln, always the politician, is quick to add that other Christian denominations also held his belief in "necessity."

Lincoln also asserts that he has not spoken against "religion in general" or "any denomination of Christians in particular." It is important to note the two qualifiers in both statements: "in general" and "in particular." Religion in its most general sense could mean the golden rule and morality. As Volney asserted, morality was the only "demonstrable part of religion." And while Lincoln may not have attacked specific sects, Christianity as a whole definitely came in for criticism.[12]

A candidate's religious beliefs were not entirely a public matter, according to Lincoln. He makes a point of "Leaving the higher matter of eternal consequences between him and his maker." As one scholar put it, "When it came to religion, Lincoln was an open-minded man who regarded the entire subject as a matter of individual conscience." Lincoln does posit one litmus test for office in saying that he could not support an "open enemy" or "scoffer" of religion. The qualifier is again important here. "Open" and "scoffer" refer to public acts, not private views. Lincoln writes that no one had the right to "insult the feelings" of a community. He may have also been just stating the fact that anyone who did this in frontier Illinois or probably anywhere else in America would never be elected.[13]

The handbill is in many ways ambiguous, probably intentionally. Those who were well disposed toward Lincoln and likely to vote for him could find what they wanted in the document. Only with additional knowledge of Lincoln's views in this period do the many ambiguities become obvious. Lincoln, who was called "honest Abe" for a reason, would not tell an outright lie, but could emphasize certain things over others because they were more palatable.

The most persuasive and clearest evidence of Lincoln's rejection of Christian orthodoxy comes from three political and personal associates: John Todd Stuart, James Matheny, and Jesse Fell. These were substantial citizens, not given to lying. Their testimony is clear and convincing. All three tell substantially the same story.

If any man could claim to have "discovered" Lincoln it was John Todd Stuart. Often that title goes to Denton Offutt, the man who had hired Lincoln to take a flatboat to New Orleans and later employed him at New Salem. But without Stuart it is arguable whether Lincoln would have ever started on his journey to greatness. Stuart's everlasting credit is he saw in the gangly and unpolished Lincoln enormous talent and potential. Stuart can truly claim to have been Lincoln's "political mentor."[14]

They first met during the Black Hawk War in 1832. They both were young, Lincoln a twenty-three-year-old captain and Stuart a twenty-five-year-old major. They were both Whigs and were run-

ning for election to the state legislature. Stuart won and Lincoln lost for
his only time by a direct vote of the
people. In 1834 Lincoln tried again.
The system was set up so that when
the votes were counted only the top
four vote-getters would go to the state
capital, so the Democrats hatched a
plan and approached Lincoln. They
would have two of their own candidates drop out and concentrate their
votes on Lincoln and the other
Democrats, thus hoping to "squeeze
out John T. Stuart." Stuart was confident of his own popularity and gra-

John Todd Stuart, Mary Todd
Lincoln's cousin and Abraham
Lincoln's law partner, pho-
tographed in 1848. (*Picture
Library* MES20734)

ciously told Lincoln to accept the offer. Stuart remembered, "I
believe he did so. I and my friends, knowing their tactics, then con-
centrated our fight against one of their men." Stuart was right to be
confident since both he and Lincoln were elected. Stuart then further extended his generosity toward Lincoln by encouraging him
to study law, which consisted of Lincoln getting his hands on a few
law books and reading them over and over on his own, and taking
him in as a law partner and splitting their fees equally.[15]

Lincoln's romantic troubles caused him to break down in the
early part of 1841. He broke off his engagement to Mary Todd
toward the end of 1840. Lincoln had his doubts about the marriage, but they were increased when he was smitten by the beautiful and pious eighteen-year-old Matilda Edwards, a cousin of
Mary's in-laws. While Lincoln probably never actively courted
Matilda, he was racked by guilt. However, he trusted Stuart
enough to unburden himself. "I am now the most miserable man
living. If what I feel were equally distributed to the whole human

family, there would not be one cheerful face on the earth. Whether I shall ever be better I can not tell; I awfully forebode I shall not. To remain as I am is impossible; I must die or be better, it appears to me." Lincoln signed the letter, "Your friend, as ever." For Lincoln to allow another into his personal pain required a high level of trust, which Stuart apparently had earned.[16]

What Stuart said of Lincoln's religion is stark and unequivocal. A year and a half after Lincoln's death he told Herndon, "Mr Lincolns Religion as I understand was of a low order—he was an infidel Especially when young—Say from 1834 to 1840." A few years later he gave a fuller statement: "I Knew Mr Lincoln when he first came here and for years afterwards—he was an avowed and open Infidel—Sometimes bordered on atheism . . . Lincoln went further against Christian beliefs - & doctrines & principles than any man I ever heard: he shocked me. . . . Suppose it was against the inherent defects so-called of the Bible & on grounds of rea-son—Lincoln always denied that Jesus was the Christ of God." Stuart later went on to mention a man who would have a profound effect on Lincoln's religious thought. He said, "The Revd Doct Smith who wrote you a letter tried to Convert Lincoln from Infidelity so late as 1858 and Couldn't do it." The first part of the statement agrees with what is known about Lincoln's views. The part about Reverend Smith is hard to tell. (Smith's importance to Lincoln's religious development is discussed in Chapter 3.) Stuart, who had moved away from Lincoln politically in the 1850s, is giv-ing either hearsay or his own educated guess of what Lincoln believed. He does not say, "Lincoln told me that Rev. Smith." Stuart was apparently unsure about Smith because he would mod-ify his opinion of Smith's effect on Lincoln a few years later.[17]

The second man who knew Lincoln well was James H. Matheny. Matheny first met Lincoln at New Salem, but was on closer terms with him in Springfield. He was the best man at

Lincoln's wedding in 1842 and an old Whig associate. Like Stuart he too differed with Lincoln in politics in the 1850s. He supported the anti-immigrant Know-Nothing Party in the 1856 election. However, he did come to support Lincoln after the Dred Scott decision of the Supreme Court in 1857.[18]

Matheny was close to Lincoln in the 1840s and heard his religious views, and like Stuart, did not pull any punches in recounting them. Matheny would sit around with Lincoln and others to discuss politics and other issues. Of Lincoln's religion, Matheny spoke a number of times. Herndon, shortly after Lincoln's death, jotted down in his usual choppy style a series of interviews with Matheny. Matheny told him, "Revelation—Virgin Mary say in 1837—8—9&c His was the language of respect yet it was from the point of ridicule—not scoff—as I once loosely Said." Matheny then told Herndon about how he and Lincoln were both clerks in Springfield in 1837, shortly after Lincoln arrived. They became friends and Matheny remembered Lincoln doing something shocking. He recalled, "That Lincoln . . . would talk about Religion—pick up the Bible—read a passage—and then Comment on it—show its falsity—and its follies on the grounds of *Reason*—would then show its own self made & self uttered Contradictions and would in the End—finally ridicule it and as it were Scoff at it."[19]

A few years later Matheny amplified his statement to Herndon on Lincoln's religious views. He remembered that Lincoln would call Christ a "bastard." Lincoln also "bordered on absolute Atheism." Matheny believed the Scottish poet Robert Burns helped Lincoln become an "infidel." He said, "—at least he found in Burns a like thinker & feeler. Lincoln quoted Tom O'Shanter [Matheny means "Holy Willie's Prayer"]—'What send one to Heaven and him to Hell all & c.'" Matheny was shocked at all this because he was "a young man & believed what my good Mother told me." Matheny also remembered Lincoln talking about his writing a religious book from New Salem: "Mr Lincoln did tell me *that he did write* a little Book on Infidelity. This Statement I have avoided heretofore, but as you strongly insist on it probably to defend yourself against charges of misrepresentation I give it to you as I got it from Lincoln's own mouth."[20]

Though Matheny does not give exact dates when Lincoln argued against the logic of the Bible, he implies that it was early on in the period of "1834-1840." Later he claims Lincoln was more "discrete" about it. Matheny later came up with a theory about why Lincoln was less open about what he called his infidelity, or unorthodoxy. Matheny assumed it was done for political reasons, but it is equally likely that Matheny was unaware that Lincoln's views may have changed. Matheny is also careful to say that when Lincoln "scoffed," he didn't mean that Lincoln was inherently dis-respectful. Instead Lincoln would appear to be ridiculing not so much the Bible but more the naïveté of many around him who took every word to be *literally* true.

The third person who gave testimony about Lincoln's religion was Jesse W. Fell, best known for asking Lincoln for a short biography to use in the eastern states where Lincoln was unknown for the 1860 election. Fell also worked hard for Lincoln's Presidential nomination at the Republican National Convention at Chicago in 1860. Fell had known Lincoln since 1834, and unlike Stuart and Matheny, had never moved away from Lincoln politically. Fell probably looms larger in Lincoln biographies than he warrants due to his statements on Lincoln's religion. Herndon relied on them extensively to paint his picture of Lincoln's skepticism. In fact, Herndon reprinted in his biography much of what Fell told Ward Hill Lamon in an 1870 letter: "I have not hesitation whatever in Saying, that whilst he held many opinions in common with the great mass of Christian believers, *he did not* believe in what are

regarded as the orthodox or evangelical views of Christianity." Fell
went on to describe how Lincoln's opinions were "utterly at vari-
ance with what are usually taught in the Churches" in regards to
things such as the "atonement," "future rewards & punishments,
and the "infallibility of the written revelation." Fell summed up
Lincoln's religious thought this way, "His religious views were emi-
nently practical, and are Summed up in these two propositions,
'the Fatherhood of God, and the Brotherhood of Man.' He fully
believed in a Superintending & overruling Providence, that guides
& controls the operations of the world; but Maintained that Law
and Order, & not their violation or suspension; are the appointed
means by which this providence is exercised."[21]

Fell believed that the theologian that best represented
Lincoln's views was Theodore Parker, a Unitarian. Fell was the
founder of the Unitarian Church in Bloomington, and he even
thought that, had things in his life turned out differently, he would
have become a Unitarian minister. This may account for a certain
bias; Fell may be converting Lincoln to Unitarianism after the fact.
There is no doubt, however, that Fell had conversations with
Lincoln regarding religion and the failings, as they saw it, of orthodox Christianity.[22]

Taken together, the testimonies of Stuart, Matheny, and Fell
show a consistent picture of Lincoln's views in New Salem and
much of his years in Springfield. They show a man who would
study the Bible, but not accept it as divinely inspired truth in all
cases. Lincoln obliquely made this point in a speech about the
Whig candidate for President, Zachary Taylor, in Congress in
1848. Lincoln wrote about the well-known differences in the
accounts of Christ's passion in the four Gospels, but later crossed
it out probably for fear of offending sensitive ears. Comparing
Taylor to Thomas Jefferson, he wrote, "They are more alike than
the accounts of the crucifixion, as given by any two of the evangel-

ists—more alike, or at least as much alike, as any two accounts of the inscriptions, written and erected by Pilate at the time." The testimonies of Stuart, Matheny, and Fell also show a man who believes in God, with occasional doubts, but accepts almost none of the trappings of Christian doctrine such as miracles, heaven and hell, and the virgin birth.[23]

LINCOLN'S ASSOCIATES OFTEN REMARKED on his melancholy and sad nature. Some felt it was the result of his lack of belief in much of Christianity. In a passage that was ghost-written but reflected the views of Illinois lawyer and political associate Ward Hill Lamon, that argument was made: "The fatal misfortune of his life, looking at it only as it affected him in this world, was the influence of New Salem and Springfield which enlisted him on the side of unbelief. He paid the bitter penalty in a life of misery." Herndon believed that many of the misfortunes in Lincoln's life fed his doubts, which in turn fed his sadness. Recounting many of Lincoln's hardships caused Herndon to blurt out in a letter, "Poor, patient, suffering, cross-bearing, sublime Lincoln! Did not God roll him through His furnace? Take all this . . . and you will perceive that Lincoln's work on infidelity—burnt up by his friends—was a blast, Job-like, of despair. Now does not melancholy drip from this poor man?"[24]

Ultimately Lincoln was a Victorian man, and unlike the early Enlightenment figures, many Victorian intellectuals did not regard freedom from religion as a "triumphant emancipation" from superstition. Instead it has been argued that he saw it as, "the source of what A. N. Wilson calls a 'terrible, pitiable unhappiness' and a wearying sense of 'metaphysical isolation' than can be stanched only by a submission to 'impersonal and unrecompensing law.'" Like many intellectuals of his time such as John Stuart

Mill, Lincoln may have felt that something precious was lost with the loss of religious faith.[25]

Whether or not it was the result of a lack of religious faith, Lincoln's melancholy was one of his most prominent traits. Herndon's literary partner Jesse Weik recalled, "Almost every man in Illinois I met, including not only Herndon, but John T. Stuart, Samuel H. Treat, James C. Conkling, James H. Matheny, David Davis, Leonard Swett, and Henry C. Whitney, reminded me of it." This impressive list of Lincoln's closest associates and other evidence has led one scholar of Lincoln's psychology to conclude, "No aspect of Lincoln's character has become more tangibly real in the literature than his sad, gloomy, melancholy appearance."[26]

The evidence suggests that Lincoln's depressions were in part related to his early lack of religious faith, in particular, to his disbelief in an afterlife. This argument was made strongly by Robert Bruce in a brilliant essay entitled "The Riddle of Death." Bruce writes, "whereas he shared with the larger, literate society of his day its emotional reaction to death, but not its refuge in an elaborately detailed and homelike heaven of reunion. In short, he rejected the chief defense of each against the terror of oblivion." The principal scholar of Lincoln's psychology also sees death playing the most prominent role in Lincoln's depression: "Lincoln's depressions probably stemmed from a series of childhood losses which included the death of his newborn younger brother when Lincoln was about three years old; the death of his mother, along with her aunt and uncle, when he was nine; and the death of his sister when he was eighteen." Lincoln as a young man lost people whom he loved, and they were gone forever; they were not waiting to meet him again in heaven.[27]

This was probably true of Lincoln's most famous episode of depression. On August 25, 1835, the twenty-two-year-old woman he had come to an understanding to marry, Ann Rutledge, died of typhoid fever. Almost all of New Salem remembered him as being inconsolable. Two witnesses recall him breaking down when it rained shortly afterward, and saying that he couldn't accept the rain or snow falling on her grave. To the young Lincoln all that was left of the woman he loved was her body in the ground. While Lincoln would remember her the rest of his life, there was no soul living on after her.[28]

The theme of death abounds in the melancholy poetry Lincoln loved. From his early copying of Calvinist verses in his copybook to his frequent reading of Robert Burns, Lincoln had an almost unquenchable thirst for somber themes in poetry. His favorite poem was the Scots poet William Knox's "Mortality." Lincoln first read the poem at New Salem in 1831 when it was introduced to him by a physician. He said of it in 1846, "I would give all I am worth, and go in debt, to be able to write so fine a piece as I think that is." He even inserted a portion of it in his eulogy of President Zachary Taylor in 1850, and ten years later he told Lamon the poem "sounded to him as much like true poetry as anything that he had ever heard." As late as 1864 Lincoln could recite the entire poem from memory. The verses resonated with Lincoln's sense of the finality of death:

> Oh! why should the spirit of mortal be proud?
> Like a swift-fleeting meteor, a fast flying cloud
> A flash of the lightning, a break of the wave
> He passeth from life to his rest in the grave.
>
> The leaves of the oak and the willow shall fade,
> Be scattered around, and together be laid;
> And the young and the old, and the low and the high,
> Shall moulder to dust, and together shall lie.

The infant a mother attended and loved;
The mother that infant's affection who proved;
The husband, that mother and infant who blest,—
Each, all, are away to their dwellings of rest.

The poem continues in such a vein for ten more stanzas and closes with:

'T is the wink of an eye—'t is the draught of a breath—
From the blossom of health to the paleness of death
From the gilded saloon to the bier and the shroud:—
Oh! Why should the spirit of mortal be proud?[29]

Other poems and songs with mortality as a theme caught Lincoln's fancy as well. Herndon remembers he had a "great fondness" for Oliver Wendell Holmes's "The Last Leaf:"

The mossy marbles rest
On the lips he has pressed
In their bloom;
And the names he loved to hear
Have been carved for many a year
On the tomb.[30]

Matheny mentioned that Burns's "Holy Willie's Prayer" helped make Lincoln an "infidel." Ample evidence shows Lincoln loved the Scottish poet. Lincoln first read Burns in Indiana, but as late as 1860 was thrilled when an acquaintance of his had met Burns's sister. Lincoln said that the man "must tell me something about her when we meet again." When Lincoln was asked to attend the annual Burns Club of Washington's dinner in 1865, he was forced to decline. When asked instead to make a toast, Lincoln could only write, "I can not frame a toast to Burns. I can say nothing worthy of his generous heart and transcending genius. Thinking of what he has said, I can not say anything worth saying."[31]

It is easy to see why "Holy Willie's Prayer" was so favored by Lincoln. It is the supposed prayer of a drunken man who, thinking that he is one of the "elect" chosen by God for salvation, feels immense pride and satisfaction knowing others are going to hell:

> O Thou, who in the heavens does dwell,
> Who, as it pleases best Thysel',
> Sends ane to heaven an' ten to hell,
> A' for Thy glory,
> And no for ony gude or ill
> They've done afore Thee!
>
> I bless and praise Thy matchless might,
> When thousands Thou hast left in night,
> That I am here afore Thy sight,
> For gifts an' grace
> A burning and a shining light
> To a' this place.
>
> What was I, or my generation,
> That I should get sic exaltation,
> I wha deserve most just damnation
> For broken laws,
> Five thousand years ere my creation,
> Thro' Adam's cause?
>
> When frae my mither's womb I fell,
> Thou might hae plunged me in hell,
> To gnash my gums, to weep and wail,
> In burnin lakes,

Where damned devils roar and yell,
Chain'd to their stakes.

Yet I am here a chosen sample,
To show thy grace is great and ample;
I'm here a pillar o' Thy temple,
Strong as a rock,
A guide, a buckler, and example,
To a' Thy flock.

Burns closes the poem with Willie thanking God but at the same time imploring him not to accept the prayers of his enemies:

Lord, in Thy day o' vengeance try him,
Lord, visit them wha did employ him,
And pass not in Thy mercy by 'em,
Nor hear their pray'r,
But for Thy people's sake, destroy 'em,
An' dinna spare.

But, Lord, remember me an' mine
Wi' mercies temp'ral an' divine,
That I for grace an' gear may shine,
Excell'd by nane,
And a' the glory shall be thine,
Amen, Amen![32]

The first verse points the illogic of a just God sending ten people to hell and one "elected" to go to heaven for God's own "glory." To Lincoln's mind this was a base injustice and served no real purpose for humanity. Lincoln probably saw the views of his contemporaries in Willie's beliefs. The sense of pride of the supposed "elect" was leading them to a false sense of superiority over their fellow man. To Lincoln, always a thorough egalitarian, this offended his belief that all should have an equal chance in life.

Lincoln himself turned to poetry after he visited his childhood home in Indiana during his electioneering. His 1846 composition "My Childhood Home I See Again" combines the theme of the finality of death and melancholy that were so much of a part of Lincoln's youth and psyche:

> My childhood-home I see again,
> And gladden with the view;
> And still as mem'ries crowd my brain,
> There's sadness in it too.
>
> O memory! thou mid-way world
> 'Twixt Earth and Paradise,
> Where things decayed, and loved ones lost
> In dreamy shadows rise.
>
> And freed from all that's gross or vile,
> Seem hollowed, pure, and bright,
> Like scenes in some enchanted isle,
> All bathed in liquid light.

Lincoln goes on about what time has done to his boyhood home:

> Now twenty years have passed away,
> Since here I bid farewell
> To woods, and fields, and scenes of play
> And school-mates loved so well.
>
> Where many were, how few remain
> Of old familiar things!
> But seeing these to mind again
> The lost and absent brings.

The friends of I left that parting day—
How changed, as time has sped!
Young childhood grown, strong manhood grey,
And half of all are dead.

I hear the lone survivors tell
How nought from death can save,
Till every sound appears a knell,
And every spot a grave.

I range the fields with pensive tread,
And pace the hollow rooms;
And feel (companions of the dead)
I'm living in the tombs.[33]

Lincoln wrote another poem a few months later about Matthew Gentry, a boy he had known in Indiana who had gone insane. In the last verse Lincoln personifies the power of death in highly laudatory terms:

O death! Thou awe-inspiring prince,
That keepst the world in fear;
Why dost thou tear more blest ones hence,
And leave him ling'ring here?[34]

Lincoln supposedly wrote an anonymous poem about suicide and had it published in the *Sangamo Journal*. A tantalizing clue comes from Herndon jotting, "Lincoln on Suicide—about 1840—See Journal 1840" in an interview with Speed a few months after Lincoln's death. It may have been the first thing Speed said to him since it is first in Herndon's notes. In a later letter Speed wrote, "My recollection is that the Poem on Suicide was written in the Spring of 1840. or Summer of 1841." Speed must have corrected his recollection of dates, because a few years later Herndon wrote, "As to the Lincoln poem on suicide I found out from Speed that it was written in 1838, and I hunted up the *Journal* and found where the poem was, what day published, etc., etc., but someone had cut it out—supposed to be Lincoln." Lincoln would have had ample opportunity to remove the poem from the files of the paper since he was good friends with its editor and often wrote for the paper.[35]

Richard Lawrence Miller, a Lincoln researcher, shed new light on this matter when he discovered an anonymous poem entitled, "The Suicide's Soliloquy" in the issue of August 25, 1838. The date of the poem opens up more questions; it was published exactly three years to the day after Ann Rutledge's death. Did Lincoln time the publication to the anniversary of Ann's tragic death? It is tantalizing to think it was not merely a coincidence.[36]

The poem itself is accompanied by a note saying that it was found "near the bones" of a corpse along the banks of the Sangamon River. The poem reads:

> Here, where the lonely hooting owl
> Sends forth his midnight moans,
> Fierce wolves shall o'er my carcase growl,
> Or buzzards pick my bones.
>
> No fellow-man shall learn my fate,
> Or where my ashes lie;
> Unless by beasts drawn round their bait,
> Or by the ravens' cry.
>
> Yes! I've resolved the deed to do,
> And this place to do it:
> This heart I'll rush a dagger through
> Though I in hell should rue it!
> Hell! What is hell to one like me

Who pleasures never knew;
By friends consigned to misery,
By hope deserted too?

To ease me of this power to think,
That though my bosom raves,
I'll headlong leap from hell's high brink
And wallow in the waves.

Though devils yells, and burning chains
May waken long regret;
Their frightful screams, and piercing pains,
Will help me to forget.

Yes! I'm prepared, through endless night,
To take this fiery berth!
Think not with tales of hell to fright
Me, who am damn'd on earth!

Sweet steel! Come forth from out of your sheath,
And glist'ning, speak your powers;
Rip up the organs of my breath,
And draw my blood in showers!

I strike! It quivers in that heart
Which drives me to this end;
I draw and kiss the bloody dart,
My last—my only friend![37]

Did Lincoln really write these verses? Joshua Wolf Shenk, a student of Lincoln's depression, states why they probably were his. "The reasons are, first, that it fits Joshua Speed's date; second, that in its syntax, tone, reasoning, and references are characteristic of

Lincoln; and third, that the poem has the same meter as Lincoln's other published verse. A number of scholars who have closely studied Lincoln in this period say the poem rings true."[38]

The poem offers no hope of a joyous afterlife. Even in death the narrator has no escape from his misery since he will "rue" what he has done in "hell." Even the torment he would supposedly suffer with "burning chains" is acceptable because it will help him "forget." The evidence is that Lincoln did not believe in heaven and hell during this period of his life, but being brought up in the Christian tradition, he was aware that suicide is considered a mortal sin. Lincoln may not have thought in those terms, but he probably saw suicide as the ultimate crime against "reason."

Lincoln's view of the hopelessness of the human condition led to his depression and gloom. This also helped Lincoln strive to achieve; he felt the only true immortality was in gaining fame by leaving the world a better place.

By 1849 Lincoln's religious views, though somewhat muddled, seemed stable. What he may have been by definition is not exactly clear. He was not an atheist in the classic sense of the term, yet he was not a Christian, either. As one Lincoln scholar has written, "There were moments when God ceased to be a person at all in Lincoln's thinking, but instead became simply 'a Superintending & overruling Providence, that guides and controls the operations of the world.'" Lincoln told the mother of a friend, "Probably it is to be my lot to go on in a twilight, feeling and reasoning my way through life, as a questioning, doubting Thomas did." He became reconciled with Mary Todd after the broken engagement and married her in November 1842. A chance encounter with a book in his father-in-law's library would soon challenge and ultimately change his views.[39]

Chapter 3

REVEREND SMITH'S BOOK

Mr. Lincoln said to me that when on a visit somewhere he had seen and
partially read a work of Dr. Smith on the evidences of Christianity, which
had led him to change his view of the Christian religion.
—*Thomas Lewis, January 6, 1873*

I N THE AUTUMN OF 1849 ABRAHAM LINCOLN stood fascinated in
his late father-in-law's library. For a man who once "pulled fod-
der" for three days to pay for the damage to a book about George
Washington, Robert Todd's book collection must have seemed like
an unimaginable abundance of riches. Looking over the titles,
Lincoln came across a name he recognized. The hefty volume,
published six years earlier, was by Reverend James D. Smith, the
minister of the First Presbyterian Church in Springfield, Illinois,
where he had taken the pulpit a few months before. This connection sparked Lincoln's curiosity. Lincoln picked it up and started
to page through the volume, whose title was long and formidable:
*The Christian's Defence, Containing a Fair Statement, and
Impartial Examination of the Leading Objections Urged by Infidels
Against the Antiquity, Genuineness, Credibility and Inspiration of
the Holy Scriptures; Enriched with Copious Extracts from Learned
Authors.*[1]

In late October 1849, Lincoln, his wife, and sons Robert and Edward had made the journey from Springfield, Illinois, to Lexington, Kentucky. Robert Todd, Mary's father, had just died from cholera at the age of fifty-nine. Lincoln had been thankful to his father-in-law for giving him and his wife money shortly after their marriage. A Todd family tradition has Robert saying of his daughter and son-in-law, "I only hope that Mary will make as good a wife as she has a husband." Lincoln even represented Robert Todd in a lawsuit and named his first child after him. Now Lincoln was called on to settle the estate and represent some of his in-laws in trials resulting from questions over the inheritance. The forty-year-old Lincoln stood in the Todds' family library, not knowing the book he was holding would transform his way of thinking and the course of his life.[2] The change in Lincoln's views of Christianity was important for him on a personal level and for the country during the difficult trial it would face. The role of Reverend Smith and the testimony about Lincoln's views during the decade prior to his presidency need to be studied in detail to understand exactly what happened.

If any man had the background to change Lincoln's mind about Christianity it was James Smith. They shared many similar experiences and their journeys to religious belief were alike in many ways. Smith was eleven years older than Lincoln, having been born in Glasgow, Scotland, in 1798. (Some sources place his birth in 1801, but his gravestone gives the earlier date.) The irony is strong: if two Scotsmen, Burns and Knox, helped Lincoln become an "infidel," it took another Scotsman to bring him around. Smith and Lincoln both lost their mothers in childhood. Smith's mother died giving birth to him and Lincoln's from the milk sickness. Like Lincoln, Smith was a religious skeptic in his youth, a "confirmed Deist." Smith too enjoyed poking fun at the antics of preachers. Smith apparently read the same works as

Lincoln. He wrote of his early skepticism in his *Christian's Defence*, "This opinion the writer formed from what he knew of the workings of his own heart, for he himself in early life was a Deist, from principle." He specifically mentioned that he had been "led astray by the Sophisms of Volney and Paine."[3]

Smith arrived in New York in 1820 to try his hand at business. Mirroring Lincoln's New Salem experience, he failed in this endeavor. He moved to southern Indiana in 1824 to teach school. Shortly after arriving, he attended a sermon by Rev. James Blackwell and was converted. Smith eagerly began to preach himself and was formally ordained in his native Presbyterian faith in 1829. He turned his talents to writing and editing religious works. Smith preached in Indiana, Kentucky, and Tennessee before coming to Springfield in March 1849.[4]

The genesis of his book was a debate he had in 1841 with C. G. Olmsted, the author of "The Bible and Its Own Refutation." An ardent free-thinker, Olmsted resided in Columbus, Mississippi. During the winter of 1839-1840, Smith visited Columbus and gave a series of lectures entitled "The Natures and Tendencies of Infidelity" and "The Evidences of Christianity." Olmsted's friends approached Smith with a written challenge to a public debate. The note offered to discuss the following questions: "Were the writers of the different books of the Bible inspired men? Did the facts which they detail occur? Was Jesus Christ miraculously begotten? Did he perform miracles? Did Jesus rise from the dead?" Lincoln had addressed a number of these in his book on infidelity.[5]

If Olmsted and his supporters thought Smith would turn them down, they did not know him. Smith was the consummate intellectual pugilist, relishing a good argument for its own sake. Smith asked for a delay to gather material necessary for the debate. He wrote to friends in Great Britain, receiving material such as drawings from monuments in Egypt supposedly showing Israelite laborers, thus supporting the account in Exodus. Lincoln would have appreciated Smith's preparation; it matched what he usually went through to build his important speeches.[6]

The contest of Smith versus Olmsted began in April 1841 in Columbus, and lasted eighteen nights. They alternated between opening and closing. The first would speak for an hour; the second would then speak for two, followed by a half-hour rebuttal from the first speaker. The debates were remembered as epic, almost matching the Lincoln and Douglas debate years later. Smith must have been an impressive sight on the platform. He had a large build and a "Websterian" appearance (the legendary orator Daniel Webster could be physically imposing on the stump). Smith was used to speaking to large congregations, and his voice rang out loud and authoritative during the debate. He was not a man to argue meekly for his point, using sarcasm in his arguments and not being above attacking Olmsted personally. A contemporary source sympathetic to Smith described his performance as being "well prepared" and his "arguments systematically arranged." Smith supposedly proved "the GENUINENESS, AUTHENTICITY and INSPIRATION" of the Scriptures. However the caveat had to be added that, "the defeat would have been more complete, had Mr. S. omitted some of his personal allusions, and had he suppressed his natural inclination to sarcasm. Indeed his blasts of sarcasm were truly WITHERING. His opponent, finding that he could not cope with him in this respect, retreated, and took shelter under the sympathies of his audience."[7]

Smith's performance sufficiently impressed the local Methodist Church elders that they wanted to share his powerful arguments with others in the community. They wrote him shortly after regarding the debates, "believing that their publication would do much to arrest the poisonous and destructive influence of Infidelity, and be calculated to promote Christianity and true patriotism, we respectfully request you to give them to the public, together with your other arguments, which were not delivered, so soon as you can, consistently with the difficulty and importance of the task." Smith complied and two years later, in 1843, published *The Christian's Defence* in a limited number of copies to subscribers. One was bought by Robert Todd and placed in the Todd family library where Lincoln discovered it six years later.[8]

Lincoln did not have enough time in Lexington to finish the book. When he returned on November 15, he sought out Thomas Lewis, a lawyer whose office was next to Lincoln's and an elder at Springfield's First Presbyterian Church, for more information. Lewis recalled, "Mr. Lincoln said to me that when on a visit somewhere he had seen and partially read a work of Dr. Smith on the evidences of Christianity, which had led him to change his view of the Christian religion, and he would like to get that work and finish the reading of it, and also to make the acquaintance of Dr. Smith. I . . . took Dr. Smith to Mr. Lincoln's office, Dr. Smith gave Mr. Lincoln a copy of his book, as I know, at his own request."[9]

What did Lincoln find in Smith's book (which was actually two volumes in one)? The first covered the Old Testament; the second covered the New. The style of argument would have appealed to Lincoln because of its legalistic and questioning nature. Smith was trying to rebut common arguments given by skeptics of Christianity, and probably hit on many Lincoln would have used against it in his younger days at New Salem and Springfield.

Smith begins by declaring that evidence, not emotions, should be the basis of belief. This was precisely the type of argument that appealed to Lincoln. In an 1842 temperance address Lincoln states, "Happy day, when, all appetites controled, all passions subdued, all matters subjected, *mind*, all conquering *mind*, shall live and move the monarch of the world. Glorious consummation! Hail fall of Fury! Reign of Reason, all hail!" Smith wrote, "Men are in danger of making this a question of sentiment, instead of a question of pure truth." He went on to classify people into two groups. The first group was "anxious to give every support and stability to a system which they conceive to be most intimately connected with the dearest hopes and wishes of humanity, may feel disposed to overrate its evidences." The second group, in contrast, was likely to "view the claims of Revelation as superstitious folly, and feel that they are descending, when they bring their attention to a subject which engrosses so much respect and admiration from the vulgar; thereby they are disqualified, properly, to investigate its evidences." To reach a valid conclusion, Smith felt, "all references to religion must be laid aside; and the question must be viewed purely as one of erudition." Lincoln found himself in strong agreement with Smith on this point.[10]

Smith's book was published sixteen years before Charles Darwin's *On the Origin of Species*. Smith is unfairly dismissive of Darwin and other natural scientists of the day whose revolutionary discoveries were leading to great advances in human knowledge and science. Smith lists as his targets "Linnaeus, Buffon, Helvetius, Monoboddo, and Darwin" and witheringly states, "And from whom do these philosophers, thus departing from the whole letter and spirit of the Mosaic history, pretend to derive the race of man? The four former from the race of monkeys; and the last, to complete the absurdity, from the race of oysters; for Dr. Darwin seriously conjectures that as aquatic animals appear to have been produced before terrestrial."[11]

According to the Springfield tailor James W. Keyes, who knew Lincoln in the 1850s, Lincoln's views were closer to Darwin's than Smith's on these points. He recalled, "In my intercours with Mr Lincoln I learned that he believed in a Creator of all things, who had neither beginning nor end, who possessing all power and wisdom, established a principal, in Obedience to which, Worlds moved and are upheld, and animel and vegetable life came into existence." Lincoln could see the natural processes creating the earth and life on it, but as opposed to the materialistic Atheist view, he agreed with Smith that a creator had to be the source. According to Keyes, Lincoln saw the proof of this all around him. Keyes recalls, "A reason he gave for his belief was, that in view of the Order and harmony of all nature which all beheld, it would have been More miraculous to have Come

Reverend James D. Smith led the First Presbyterian Chuch of Springfield, Illinois, from 1849 to 1856. (*History of the Cumberland Presbyterian Church*)

about by chance, than to have been created and arranged by some great thinking power."[12]

Smith attempts to prove that much of what happened in the narrative in the early books of the Bible is the faithful record of events. In the 1920s William Barton would defensively say, "We need not concern ourselves with the question whether Dr. Smith's line of argument is that which probably would be found most cogent if a similar debate were to be held at the present day."[13]

Smith takes on the skeptics who argued the racist notion that all of humankind could not have descended from the same ancestors. He mentions those who think "the wide difference in form, and color and degree of intellect" make descent from a common ancestor as in the Mosaic narrative impossible. Smith, perhaps ahead of his time, argues for the similarities among humans. He in fact argues for environmental factors explaining the differences between people. He shows, "the absurdity of the argument of a plurality of human stocks or species, from a mere difference in the color of skin; an argument thus proved to be altogether superficial, and which we gravely assert to be not more than *skin-deep*." Lincoln was in sympathy with this argument; while he recognized differences between the free white and black slave, he believed that the black slave still warranted the same rights given the free white in the Declaration of Independence.[14]

Smith was no fundamentalist in his interpretation of the Bible. Unlike some Creationists, Smith did not accept that the days of creation were literal twenty-four-hour periods. He saw the strata of rock as evidence of the great age of the earth, a standard concept of geology. Smith did not believe that dinosaurs and man were on earth concurrently, as some of the more radical Creationists and Literalists do, but instead that there was a long period of time before the creation of man, during which the work of animal creation was finished, including an "age of reptiles." Smith would have been closer to those who in the present day claim that the universe shows evidence of "intelligent design."[15]

Smith was also not opposed to humans' study of nature, because he believed it would give people a greater appreciation of what God had created. He writes, "The heavens are our witnesses; earth is full of our depositories; truth must spring up where the creator hath sown it; and philosophers at last must be tributaries. . . . Knowledge shall be the stability of the times of the Messiah and the mind of man, enlightened in the knowledge of the word and works of God, shall be freed from the nebulosity which enshrouds it, and the light shall be divided from the darkness." Lincoln would have appreciated this contrast to those preachers he knew as a young man who saw the Bible as the only book worthy of study. Here Smith sees faith and reason capable of working together.[16]

The second volume of Smith's work focuses mostly on the New Testament. He starts by reprinting a manifesto of English freethinkers whose leader was an ex-clergyman, Robert Taylor. The manifesto has four propositions:

I. That the Scriptures of the New Testament, were not written by the persons whose names they bear.

II. That they did not appear in the times to which they refer.

III. That the persons of whom they treat, never existed.

IV. That the events, which they relate, never happened.

The manifesto then goes on to give evidence for its propositions.[17]

Smith concedes part of Taylor's first proposition that not all the books in the New Testament bear the correct name of the author. Smith writes, "Some also questioned the genuineness of the epistle to the Hebrews, the second epistle of Peter, the two last of John and the epistle of Jude." Yet he is quick to add, "But it is worthy of remark, that the books concerning which any doubts existed, do not in any way touch the general truth of the Gospels."[18]

Smith rebuts the second proposition with large groups of quotations from the early Church Fathers such as Clement, Polycarp, and Origen. To show the stability and age of the New Testament, he shows these Fathers accurately quoting much of it prior to the third or fourth century. Lincoln was probably impressed with this straightforward statistical analysis of quotations.[19]

Of the third proposition, Smith has nothing but contempt. The hyperskeptical position that no such person as Jesus of Nazareth ever existed was given credence by Volney. Smith is at his sarcastic best when he writes, "Mr. Volney, whose philosophy elevated him above all vulgar prejudices in favor of historical testimony, and with whom all well known laws of moral evidence had no weight, lays it down as a clear case that no such person as Jesus Christ ever lived in the world; and on that position framed a theory, which, on the pain of being ridiculed as a generation of credulous dupes, his readers were forthwith required to adopt." Smith ably rebuts this position with references to the extrabiblical accounts of Jesus and early Christianity such as those by Josephus and Tacitus.[20]

Smith devotes much space to rebutting the fourth proposition's denying the events in the New Testament. Of the witnesses to those events, Smith formulates an argument that would hold special appeal to the lawyer Lincoln. He writes, "Let us now enquire into the characters and circumstances of these men who testify of Jesus Christ. In a court of law, the weight of the testimony is judged by the character and circumstances of those who depose it. The judge, or the jury . . . examine the testimony itself; they enquire whether the unerring signs of veracity are apparent in it; whether there is that honest consistency in its different parts which are the sure marks of truth." Continuing with the analogy of a law case, he states that a judge or a jury "enquire into the moral character of the witnesses, whether their moral conduct is such as affords a pledge that their sincerity may be relied upon; whether they were in a situation to know the real truth; whether their temporal interests, their previous prejudices and habits, throw any light upon the motives by which they are governed in their testimony."[21]

Smith makes a lawyerly appeal on behalf of the Evangelists as faithful recorders of events when he states, "These witnesses were not enthusiasts or fanatics. Such persons labor under the influence of blind credulity, in consequence of which, they imagine themselves the peculiar favorites of Heaven. . . . Their faith in Christ was the result of rational conviction, not upon internal persuasion alone, but in the irrefragable evidence of clear and stupendous miracles, addressed to their senses." Then Smith echoes almost exactly Lincoln's famous 1838 Lyceum speech in which Lincoln praises "cold, calculating unimpassioned reason" and observes that "passion has helped us; but can do so no more." Smith writes, "They do not, like enthusiasts, act from the dictates of passion and imagination. Their readers are not required to believe, because they believe; but to confirm the truth of their mission and their doctrine, they appeal to facts, arguments, and miracles. . . . Their discourse on morals and religion then were, and now are, the most noble, rational, and satisfactory ever witnessed by mankind."[22]

Smith's defense of the resurrection accounts puts him at odds with one of the young Lincoln's favorite authors, Thomas Paine. In *The Age of Reason*, read by Lincoln in New Salem, Paine writes, "The story of Jesus Christ appearing after he was dead is the story of an apparition, such as timid imaginations can always create in vision, and credulity believe. Stories of this kind had been told of the assassination of Julius Caesar, not many years before; and they generally have their origin in violent deaths, or in the execution of innocent persons." Paine continues in language that it is easy to imagine Lincoln himself using: "In cases of this kind, compassion lends its aid and benevolently stretches the story. It goes on a little further till it becomes a most certain truth. Once start a ghost and credulity fills up the history of its life and assigns the cause of its appearance! One tells it one way, another, another way, till there are as many stories about the ghost and about the proprietor of the ghost, as there are about Jesus Christ in these four books."[23]

Smith will have none of this. He points to the five hundred whom the Apostle Paul mentions as having seen the risen Christ at one time shortly after the crucifixion (1 Corinthians 15:6). Smith writes, "How will the Infidel account for the fact that all these five hundred persons, to the very last, persisted in asserting, that with their own eyes they had seen Christ after his pretended resurrection?" Smith thinks it unlikely that every one of the five hundred would be deluded or a liar.[24]

Perhaps the cleverest section of Smith's work is that in which he uses Volney's words as evidence against that writer's own arguments. This must have especially appealed to Lincoln's sense of humor. Volney was highly skeptical of the notion of the divine inspiration of prophecy in the Bible. Smith lines up to the left various prophecies of the Bible and on the right the corresponding testimony of Volney to its truthfulness. For instance, Smith quotes the Old Testament, "I will *scatter you among the heathen*, and will draw out a sword after you: and *your land shall be desolate*" (Leviticus 36:33). Volney states in *Ruins*, "The Jews, as you all know, have been scattered among the heathen. I have traversed this *desolate* country." A prophet from the Old Testament says "The noise of them that rejoice endeth; all joy is darkened; the mirth of the land is gone" (Isaiah 23:8, 11). In Volney's *Travels*, he recounts, "They have a serious, nay, even sad and melancholy countenance. They rarely laugh; and the gayety of the French appears to them a fit of delirium." One other prophet states, "And the *cities* that are in habitable shall be laid waste, and they shall know that I am the Lord" (Ezekiel 12:20). Volney writes in *Ruins*, "Every day I found in my route villages deserted and *cities* in ruins." It is not hard to imagine Lincoln chuckling quietly as he read these parallel quotes in Smith's work.[25]

Smith then makes a last appeal to the readers. He ends his work as a lawyer would his closing arguments. He writes, "A word to the reader, and we are done. In attempting to vindicate the claims of the Bible as a revelation from God, the argument has been confined to the external evidences by which its claims are supported, and little or no notice has been taken of the internal evidences, which are peculiarly clear and convincing. We have taken nothing for granted, but have reasoned together, from the first line to the last." Smith showed his confidence in his arguments by calling on all to use reason when deciding the truth of the Christian religion by declaring, "Should he act upon this principle, we feel confident that the result must be an entire conviction that the attacks of Infidelity upon the impregnable bulwarks of Revelation, only exhibit the enmity, folly, and madness of its votaries. And that the

Bible, the more it is attacked, only shines the more brightly, and that the very objections of its enemies are converted into evidences of its truth."[26]

Lincoln might not have been convinced by all of Smith's arguments, but there is evidence that the book influenced him. Lincoln's brother-in-law Ninian Wirt Edwards attests to this in an 1872 letter: "A short time after the Rev. Dr. Smith became pastor of the First Presbyterian Church in this city, Mr. Lincoln said to me, 'I have been reading a work of Dr. Smith on the evidences of Christianity, and have heard him preach and converse on the subject, and am now convinced of the truth of the Christian religion.'" Edwards was a Whig like Lincoln in their youth and, like John Todd Stuart, had moved away from Lincoln politically, yet the family connection kept them in touch with each other. Edwards makes it clear that Lincoln's admiration of Smith's work comes from Lincoln himself.[27]

While Lincoln was reading and studying Smith's defense of the Christian religion, tragedy intervened. Shortly after the Lincolns had returned from Springfield, their second son, three-year-old Eddie, was taken ill with what was probably pulmonary tuberculosis. Both parents did what they could to nurse him, but they could not save him. He lingered for fifty-two days and died on February 1, 1850, two months shy of his fourth birthday. If a supposed photograph of Eddie, found after lying forgotten for eighty years in the drawer of Herbert Wells Fay, an early custodian of the Lincoln tomb, is genuine, and there is good reason to think it is, the Lincolns must have been especially devastated to lose such a precious child. Later, Lincoln was visibly upset when he saw the card with the doctor's last prescription for Eddie.[28]

Mary was nominally an Episcopalian, so the grief-stricken parents turned to Rev. Charles Dresser, the Episcopal minister who had married them and had sold them their house; however, he was out of town. So the Presbyterian minister, James Smith, came to the Lincolns' home and preached at the funeral the day after Eddie's death. This brought Lincoln and Smith closer. Perhaps something Smith said at the funeral led Lincoln or possibly Mary to write this poem, published anonymously in the *Illinois Daily Journal* a few days later:

> Those midnight stars are sadly dimmed,
> That late so brilliantly shone,
> And the crimson tinge from cheek and lip,
> With the heart's warm life has flown—
> The angel of Death was hovering nigh,
> And the lovely boy was called to die.
>
> The silken waves of his glossy hair
> Lie still over his marble brow,
> And the pallid lip and pearly cheek
> The presence of Death avow.
> Pure little bud in kindness given,
> In mercy taken to bloom in heaven.
>
> Happier far is the angel child
> With the harp and the crown of gold,
> Who warbles now at the Savior's feet
> The glories to us untold.
> Eddie, meet blossom of heavenly love,
> Dwells in the spirit-world above.
>
> Angel Boy—fare thee well, farewell
> Sweet Eddie, We bid thee adieu!
> Affection's wail cannot reach thee now
> Deep though it be, and true.
> Bright is the home to him now given
> For, "of such is the kingdom of Heaven."

The last line, placed on Eddie's gravestone, quoted a famous text from the New Testament. In the Gospel of Matthew, Jesus rebukes his disciples for keeping small children away from him. "But Jesus said, Permit little children, and forbid them not, to come unto me; for of such is the kingdom of heaven" (Matthew 19:14).[29]

Edward "Eddie" Baker Lincoln. (*Courtesy of Keya Morgan*)

One of the three main witnesses to Lincoln's lack of belief in his youth, John Todd Stuart, wrote to a minister in December 1872 of Smith's influence on Lincoln: "I was once interviewed on the subject of Mr. Lincoln's religious opinions, and doubtless said that Mr. Lincoln was in the earlier part of his life an infidel. I could not have said that 'Dr. Smith tried to convert Lincoln from his infidelity as late as 1858, and couldn't do it.'" Stuart then recalled the effect Eddie's death had on the Lincolns and how Smith became "intimate" with the family as a result. The effect of this, he writes, was that "Dr. Smith and Mr. Lincoln had much discussion in relation to the truth of the Christian religion, and that Dr. Smith had furnished Mr. Lincoln with books to read on that subject, and among others one which had been written by himself, some time previous, on infidelity; and that Dr. Smith claimed that after this investigation Mr. Lincoln had changed his opinion, and became a believer in the truth of the Christian religion." Stuart believed that Lincoln's honesty would have meant his change of view was genuine. He writes, "Truthfulness was a prominent trait in Mr. Lincoln's character, and it would be impossible for any intimate friend of his to believe that he ever aimed to deceive, either by his words or his conduct." (Stuart himself was mistaken about not having made his earlier claim about Dr. Smith's inability to convert Lincoln; the comment was recorded by Herndon when Stuart made it in 1870.)[30]

The second great witness to Lincoln's youthful indifference to religion was James Matheny. In 1870, Matheny told Herndon he had a theory about why Lincoln spent time with Smith. Matheny believed, "that Lincoln played a sharp game here on the Religious world—that Lincoln Knew that he was to be a great man—was a rising man—was looking to the Presidency &c. and well Knowing that the old infidel, if not Atheistic charge would be made & proved against him and to avoid the disgrace—odium and unpopularity of it tramped on the Christian toes saying—'Come and Convert me.'" By appearing as a sincere seeker of the truth, "it was noised about that Lincoln was a seeker after Salvation & in the Lord—that letters were written more or less all over the land that Lincoln was soon to be a changed man &c and thus it was he used the Revd Jas Smith of Scotland." Lincoln's "sharp game" has been accepted by some biographers, but it is actually supposition on Matheny's part. Having known Lincoln at the height of his lack of belief, Matheny may have assumed that Lincoln was simply leading Smith and others along. With his basic honesty, Lincoln would not have gone through the charade of going to church to fool ministers. Also, when Lincoln first started his conversations with Smith in late 1849, he was hardly looking to the presidency. Lincoln became serious about the presidency only after the debates of 1858 with Stephen Douglas, so even Matheny's date of 1854 is wrong. However, like Stuart, Matheny changed his tune. In 1872, he wrote, "While I do believe Mr. Lincoln to have been an infidel in his former life, when his mind was as yet unformed, and his associations principally with rough and skeptical men, yet I believe he was a very different man in later life; and that after associating with a different class of men, and investigating the subject, he was a firm believer in the Christian religion."[31]

There may have been more than meets the eye to Stuart and Matheny's "recanting." Ward Hill Lamon's biography of Lincoln was published in 1872, the year both decided to publicly correct their views on Lincoln's religion. Lamon's book, which relied heavily on Herndon's notes and interviews, used information from both Stuart and Matheny to bolster the case that Lincoln was an infidel. The book sold few copies and was savaged by critics for its unvarnished look at Lincoln's youth and for its attempt to portray Lincoln as an unbeliever. Lamon devotes much of a chapter to the testimony given Herndon on this point. Since the book was attacked, it makes sense that both Stuart and Matheny would try to distance themselves from it as much as possible. Still, their 1872 testimony is not in any sense a direct contradiction of what they told Herndon before. The Lincoln they had known was indeed an unbeliever in his youth; perhaps they felt that this emphasis on his early lack of belief by Lamon and Herndon was overdone. This was not necessarily due to political pressure; it is more likely that they wanted to clarify their views for posterity.[32]

Others reject the notion that Smith converted Lincoln. Not surprisingly, Herndon vigorously objected to this view. In an 1870 letter to Lamon, he states, "One thing is true: that the said Reverend Dr. Smith of Scotland presented Lincoln with a book written by said doctor; Lincoln brought it to the office, laid it down, never took it up again to my knowledge, never condescended to write his name in it, never spoke of it to me." Lincoln not writing his name on a book was strange to Herndon, though it probably doesn't mean much. Herndon, who owned quite a large library, would write his own name on books four or five times to show ownership. Also, Herndon's testimony is simply that he personally never saw Lincoln read it in the law office. He hardly knows of the time Lincoln studied it in Lexington and at Springfield at home. Strangely, too, Herndon soon contradicts himself in the letter by making clear he does not know of Lincoln's beliefs with any certainty. He says of Lincoln, "I know he scarcely trusted any man with his more profound secrets. I had to read them in his facts, acts, hints, face, as well *as what he did not do nor say.*" It could be too that Herndon had a grudge against Smith because of his defense of Mary Todd Lincoln and a sarcastic letter to Herndon a few years before, quoted below. Herndon makes a rather nasty character attack on Smith, insinuating that Smith is himself personally flawed by stating, "I should be compelled to say something of Smith's morals, temperance, integrity, and character generally." The conflict between the two men sheds little light on what Lincoln's beliefs actually were and instead showed Smith's arrogance and Herndon's pettiness.[33]

Lincoln's oldest son, Robert, was also unsure of Smith's influence on Lincoln. In late 1866 he wrote to Herndon, "In answer to your question I have to say that I do not know of Dr Smith having 'converted' my father from 'Unitarian' to 'Trinitarian' belief, nor do I know that he held any decided views on the subject as I never heard him speak of it." It is pertinent to remember however that Robert was only six years old when Eddie died and would not have known Lincoln's religious views before that time. It is also clear from what Robert writes that he did not hold deep theological discussions with his father on the divinity of Christ. In addition, Robert was away at Harvard and then in the army on Grant's staff during Lincoln's Presidency and did not have the opportunity for close relations with his father. Robert was twenty-two when Lincoln died and might have been able to give a fuller picture had Lincoln lived.[34]

Conversely, Lincoln's wife affirms Smith's influence on Lincoln. Twenty years after the funeral service of Eddie, Mary gave testimony in a letter to Smith, "From the time of the death of our little Edward, I believe my husband's heart, was directed towards religion & as time passed on—when Mr Lincoln became elevated to Office—with the care of a great Nation upon his shoulders— when devastating war was upon us—then indeed to my own knowledge—did his great heart go up daily, hourly, in prayer to God—for his sustaining power." Mary was letting Smith know that the time he came into Lincoln's life, at the death of Eddie, was a turning point for Lincoln's religious development. Much happened to Mary in the twenty years after Eddie died, but she could still be appreciative of what Smith had done for them. It is possible that Mary was writing merely what Smith wanted to hear. Smith had done a great deal for Mary after Lincoln's death by acting as her protector against some of the testimony about Lincoln's early love for Ann Rutledge. Smith was wrong on the facts of this portion of Lincoln's life, but Mary appreciated his defense. It would be hard, though, to call Mary's testimony a wholesale invention, since it matches up with others who state Lincoln was impressed by Smith's arguments in favor of Christianity around the time of Eddie's death.[35]

Mary was so thankful to Smith for his funeral sermon for Eddie that she converted to Presbyterianism two years after Eddie's death. Not much should be read into the fact that Lincoln was not present when Mary joined. He was in court at Urbana that day, for he was on the legal circuit most Sundays. Nor should too much be made of his lack of membership in a church, since in 1860 it is estimated that only 23 percent of the free American population was an actual member of a church. Lincoln donated money to the church and paid the fifty-dollar annual fee plus the assessed tax to rent pew No. 20. Lincoln would sometimes attend Sunday services with Mary and the children, and in 1855, the Lincolns' youngest son, Tad, was baptized in the church.[36]

What did Smith have to say about his own assessment of his work with Lincoln? In an 1867 letter to Herndon he makes it clear that he is proud of what he accomplished. The old sarcastic fire which must have animated him in his debates with Olmsted more than twenty-five years earlier is still present. Much of the letter is devoted to the impropriety of Herndon bringing up the Ann Rutledge matter, but there are large sections on Lincoln's religious views. Smith writes, "Mr. Lincoln did avow his belief in the Divine Authority and Inspiration [of] the Scriptures; and I hold that it is a matter of the last importance . . . that this avowal on his part and the circumstances attending it, together with other very interested incidents, illustrative of the excellence of his character . . . should be made Known to the public." Smith then rather bombastically puts Herndon's claims to have intimate knowledge of Lincoln in their place. Smith refers to himself as "the honored instrument of bringing them from darkness to light." He continues, "A law office is by no means the best field for judging the Characters of each other by those who are brought in Contact there. No Sir. It is in the family Circle that man exhibits himself as he really is." Smith says his credentials are much better than Herndon's in judging a man's faith in that as a minister he "has buried their dead and baptized their living: who in seasons of sorrows had administered to them, those Consolations which the Gospel of the Son of God can alone Communicate. . . . This is the man who provided he possesses understanding and judgment above all others is prepared to put a true estimate upon the Characters of each of the members of such a family."[37]

Smith then narrates the effects his *Christian's Defence* had on Lincoln. He writes his letter "is the Vindication of the Character of the Martyred president, from the foul aspersions, You sir have Cast upon it, and by the person whose high honor it was to place before Mr. Lincoln arguments designed to prove the Divine authority of the Scriptures accompanied by the arguments of Infidel objectors in their own language. To the arguments on both sides Mr. Lincoln gave a most patient, impartial and Searching investigation." Smith was sure Lincoln was convinced. He told Herndon, "To use his own language 'he examined the Arguments as a lawyer who is anxious to reach the truth investigates testimony.' The result was the announcement by himself that the argument in favor of the Divine Authority and inspiration of the Scripture was unanswerable." Smith pulls out all the stops to tell Herndon, "I Could say much on this Subject but as you are the person addressed for the present I decline. This much however:— the preparation of that work Cost me long and arduous mental labor, and if No other effect was ever produced by it, than the influence it exerted upon the mind of that man whose name thrills the heart of every patriotic American, I thank God that I was induced to undertake the work." Despite his sarcasm, Smith could well be proud of the effect his book had on Lincoln. His work caused Lincoln at the least to pause to consider the arguments in favor of the Christian religion.[38]

Lincoln himself wrote about the change in his view of the afterlife. Less than a year following Eddie's death, Lincoln's father lay dying in Coles County, Illinois. Lincoln had already rushed to see his father two years before, when it was assumed he was dying. Now Lincoln had trouble getting there because Mary was sick after the birth of their third son, Willie. Lincoln wrote his stepbrother to tell their father "to remember to call upon, and confide in, our great, and good, and merciful Maker; who will not turn away from him in any extremity. He notes the fall of a sparrow, and numbers the hairs of our heads; and He will not forget the dying man, who puts his trust in Him . . . if it be his lot to go now, he will soon have a joyous [meeting] with many loved ones gone before; and where [the rest] of us, through the help of God, hope ere-long [to join] them." Many biographers have seen this letter as the ultimately insincere effort to comfort a dying man with beliefs Lincoln himself did not hold. However, those biographers have not put the letter in the context of Eddie's death and Lincoln's reading of Smith. The same thoughts that may have consoled Thomas Lincoln were also comforting Lincoln himself at the time.[39]

By the same token, Smith was not able to convince Lincoln of the orthodox Christian concept of eternal punishment in the afterlife, a key component of nineteenth-century Christian faith. Lincoln's logical mind still could not reconcile the concept of a just God foreordaining people to hell. Lincoln told another lawyer, William H. Hanna, his beliefs about this matter. Hanna later wrote to Herndon that around 1856, Lincoln "told him he was a Kind of universalist—That he could never bring himself to belief in Eternal Punishment—That men lived but a little while here & that if eternal punishment were man's doom that he should spend that little life in vigilant & ceaseless preparation—by never Ending prayer—." Lincoln would expound upon this same universalist idea a few years later to an old New Salem friend.[40]

Lincoln had further dealings with Smith throughout the 1850s. In 1853 Lincoln attended a lecture that Smith gave on temperance, "A Discourse on the Bottle—Its Evils, and the Remedy: A Vindication of the Liquor-Seller, and the Liquor Drinker, from Certain Aspirations Cast upon Them by Many." Smith's key text is from the Old Testament: "Woe unto him that giveth his neighbor drink, that puttest thy wineskin to *him*, and makest him drunk" (Habakkuk 2:15). He states, "it is the duty of all who have in any way contributed to place temptation before him [the 'inebriate'], as an act of justice to the wronged, to labor for his emancipation from his cruel thraldom. Until this be done, that aweful woe in the text must rest upon us as a people, for in the sight of God, we are all guilty." Lincoln was so impressed that he joined with thirty-eight others in issuing a request that Smith's lecture be published.[41]

While Lincoln, like Smith, supported temperance, he was unlike Smith in that he did not support prohibition. However, as one scholar points out, the main area of agreement was "First and foremost, in the preacher's refusal to turn a blind eye to the culpability of those who are quick to assign all blame to the sellers and drinkers of liquor." Lincoln had said as much in his own temperance lecture delivered more than ten years before: "Too much denunciation against dram sellers and dram-drinkers was indulged in. This, I think, was both impolitic and unjust."[42]

The records of Smith's Presbyterian Church hold but one reference to Lincoln. In the minutes of an April 26, 1853, meeting, he was to represent the church regarding payments for a church organ in a lawsuit that was eventually dropped. In the minutes the trustees refer to Lincoln not just as a member of the church but as a member of the "congregation," thus implying Lincoln contributed enough and attended enough of the time he was in Springfield to earn that distinction. Lincoln supposedly also gave a lecture on the Bible in the church. While Lincoln may have made a few remarks on the Bible, the notion that he delivered an entire lecture is doubtful, because such an address from so prominent a citizen in the 1850s would have left a record. It may also be that memories conflated the fact that in 1858 Lincoln did give a lecture on "Discoveries and Inventions" which employed numerous quotations from the Old Testament in tracing humanity's advancement. That speech was given in a number of towns.[43]

Smith visited the Lincoln home and sometimes shared a carriage with Mary Todd Lincoln. He left Springfield in 1856 for Chicago to take a position with the American Sunday School Union. Smith had been involved in educational projects for some time, so this move was a natural one. Mary thought she knew the real reason. She wrote a relative, "Dr Smith, who finding his salary of some $1,600 inadequate, has resigned the church." Smith did probably ask for more money, yet this was likely not the main reason for leaving. Mary could have been projecting her own irrational obsession with money and poverty after Lincoln's death onto Smith.[44]

With the elevation of Lincoln to the White House, Smith continued his association with him and his family. Even though Smith was a Democrat and had originally moved to the South and preached in Kentucky and Tennessee after leaving Scotland, he stayed loyal to the Union during the war. In June 1861, he visited the Lincolns at the White House and took up temporary residence. Smith's wife was unwell, and he wanted employment. Lincoln, to avoid the political fallout of giving another Springfield friend a position, appointed Smith's son, Hugh, as American counsel in Scotland at Dundee. Smith accompanied his son back to his native land. In early 1862, Hugh became ill and returned to America; Lincoln, after some jockeying by others to get the job, gave it to Smith, who was in Scotland when Lincoln was assassinated. Robert Todd Lincoln made sure Andrew Johnson allowed Smith to keep his job as a favor to the old family friend. Mary and Tad Lincoln visited Smith in 1869, and she gave him one of Lincoln's golden canes as a memento, which he in turn willed to the English Liberal politician and Lincoln admirer John Bright. Smith became ill in 1870 of typhoid fever and died the next year. His epitaph was "A Sinner Saved by Grace."[45]

SMITH DID MORE THAN ANY OTHER INDIVIDUAL to shape Lincoln's religious thinking toward a more favorable view of Christianity. His book, though forgotten now, was an integral part of that transformation. His background as a religious skeptic in his youth allowed him to speak a language Lincoln understood. His influence is readily seen in Lincoln's 1859 interview with an old New Salem friend.

Isaac Cogdal was living in New Salem when Lincoln arrived in 1831. Three years later he bought a piece of property that was surveyed by Lincoln. Cogdal was tall and good-looking; he worked as a brick and stone mason until an explosion in a rock quarry blew off his left arm. Lincoln encouraged his friend to study law, and even in his own law office. Cogdal had a close relationship with Lincoln which allowed him to discuss with President-elect Lincoln the old days and the people they knew in 1861. Lincoln was confident enough to talk with Cogdal about his early love for Ann Rutledge, something he didn't mention to many.[46]

Two years before this Lincoln had talked to Cogdal about religion. When Cogdal had first met Lincoln, Lincoln was at the height of his lack of belief, but by 1859 that had changed. Cogdal described an interview he had with Lincoln that year to a politician and acquaintance, B. F. Irwin, in an 1874 letter. He wrote, "He did not nor could not believe in the endless punishment of any one of the human race. He understood punishment for sin to be a Bible doctrine; but that the punishment was parental in its object, aim, and design and intended for the good of the offender; hence it must cease when justice is satisfied. He added all that was lost by the transgression of Adam was made good by the atonement, all that was lost by the fall was made good by the sacrifice." Lincoln then told Cogdal, "that punishment was a provision of the gospel system, he was not sure but the world would be better off if a little more punishment was preached by our ministers, and not so much pardon for sin." When Cogdal told Lincoln that he agreed with him and that this made Lincoln a "universalist," Lincoln replied that "he never took any part in the argument or discussion of theological questions." Cogdal's testimony should be given great weight because he told the same story to Herndon shortly after Lincoln's death. Cogdal's veracity has been under attack by many, mostly because the defenders of Mary Todd

Lincoln do not like his important testimony about Ann Rutledge that suggests Lincoln loved women other than Mary, yet Herndon was there when Cogdal spoke to Lincoln in 1859 about religion and jotted down, "This is Correct Herndon" in his record of his conversation with Cogdal.[47]

What is different from Lincoln's other religious pronouncements is that here he speaks of "atonement," meaning he sees some saving function in Christ's death. Cogdal is further supported by John Wickizer, a lawyer who knew Lincoln in the 1850s who wrote Herndon almost two years after Lincoln's death, "I think he was *naturally* religious, but very liberal in his views, I think he believed in 'Jesus Christ, and him crucified.'" If Wickizer is directly quoting Lincoln, then Lincoln saw Christ's death as important enough to qualify his belief in Jesus Christ. This has led one Lincoln scholar to state, "Though historians remain understandably cautious about Lincoln's private religion, they generally agree that it was scarcely Christ-centered (though Christ's atonement for all mankind was an essential element of his seemingly universalist theology)."[48]

If Lincoln did indeed believe this, does it say that Lincoln thought Jesus' death had some larger function? It is hard to say since Lincoln does mention God often in speeches in the 1850s as the issue of slavery came to the forefront, yet is silent on Jesus. For example, in 1856 Lincoln told a cheering crowd in Michigan, "So sure as God lives, the victory shall be yours." Writing a speech about Stephen A. Douglas's Popular Sovereignty notion, letting the people in the territories decide if they want to have slavery or not, he asked in 1859, "How long, in the government of a God, great enough to make and maintain this Universe, shall there continue knaves to vend and fools to gulp, so low a piece of [demagoguery] as this[?]" And in late 1859 at Clinton, Illinois, he stated, "But I do hope that as there is a just and righteous God in Heaven, our principles will and shall prevail sooner or later." No reference to Jesus is present in any of these speeches.[49]

THE POLITICAL ISSUES WITH WHICH THE COUNTRY struggled in the 1850s also contributed to Lincoln's religious development. The Whig Party had all but disappeared in the mid-1850s. The northern and southern wings of the party had broken over the issue of slavery. After the Mexican War the United States had expanded west. Should slavery be allowed to set foot on this new soil? When Stephen Douglas and the Democrats passed the Kansas-Nebraska Act in 1854, allowing slavery to expand into territory where it had been previously banned, Lincoln was outraged. In particular, he could not stand the failure of Douglas and other Democrats to recognize that slavery was morally repugnant. Lincoln had believed that if slavery were confined to where it was constitutionally legal, it would eventually die out. Now he saw it spreading and gaining new life. The Republican Party was formed to stop the spread of slavery. Its platform called for the banning of slavery in federal territories. By 1856, Lincoln had joined the new party, and four short years later he was its first successful Presidential candidate.[50]

Lincoln's nomination for President in 1860 was an unlikely event. The Republican Party had William Seward as the front-runner for the nomination, but he was seen by many as too radical to be elected. The party turned to a much less known figure from the west in Lincoln. Although it is tempting to think of politics as somehow nobler than today, the candidates used flippant slogans, people worried about electability, and candidates had to raise money just as they do today. The campaigns could also be very negative. Personal attacks on candidates were not uncommon. Unlike in his run for Congress, religion played no real role in Lincoln's election due to overriding importance of the slavery issue.[51]

Lincoln won the election by beating three other candidates, Stephen Douglas for the northern Democrats, John Breckenridge for the southern Democrats, and John Bell who led the remnants of the old Whig Party. Lincoln got about 40 percent of the popular vote, but a majority in the Electoral College. His anti-slavery attitude was so troubling to the South that southern states started leaving the Union after his election.[52]

One highly controversial incident may shed light on Lincoln's view of Jesus just as he was about to leave for Washington. However, the controversy that has surrounded it has left many to discount the whole matter. Shortly after Lincoln's death, Josiah Holland, a journalist from Massachusetts, set out to write the first thoroughly researched biography on Lincoln. One person he interviewed was with the superintendent of Illinois education, Newton Bateman, whose office was next door to President-elect Lincoln's in the Illinois state capital building. Often Bateman would walk over and visit Lincoln. Holland describes a particular meeting of the two at length in his biography. Lincoln had picked up a book that showed what candidate the citizens of Springfield had given their intention to vote for. Lincoln called Bateman over and told him he wanted to see how the ministers would vote. Lincoln found that only three out of twenty-three intended to vote for him. According to Holland, Lincoln then made a startling statement: "'Mr. Bateman, I am not a Christian—God knows I would be one—but I have carefully read the Bible." In Holland's account, Lincoln then supposedly produced a pocket New Testament and said, "'These men well know that I am for freedom in the territories, freedom everywhere as far as the Constitution and laws will permit, and that my opponents are for slavery . . . yet, with this book in their hands, in the light of which human bondage cannot live a moment, they are going to vote against me. I do not understand it at all.'" Holland then has Lincoln saying, "I know there is

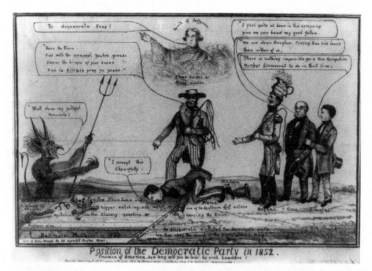

A satirical lithograph from 1852 criticizing Franklin Pierce and the Democratic party's platform of appeasing southern slavery in order to preserve the Union. (*Library of Congress*)

a God, and that He hates injustice and slavery. I see the storm coming, and I know that His hand is in it. If He has a place and work for me—and I think He has—I believe I am ready. I am nothing, but truth is everything. I know I am right because I know that liberty is right, for Christ teaches it, and Christ is God."[53]

To Holland, the reason some of Lincoln's friends did not know was that Lincoln hid it from those who disagreed with him. Holland wrote, "but the fact is a matter of history that he never exposed his own religious life to those who had no sympathy with it." Bateman understood this viewpoint. The issue of the possible bias of Holland has made many question this incident. A deeply religious man, Holland wanted Lincoln to share his views. One historian has stated that this interview was "for Holland the 'golden link in the chain of Mr. Lincoln's history,' since Bateman's claim that Lincoln had confessed the political necessity of hiding his religious convictions from public view not only put Lincoln where Holland had hoped to find him, on the side of the angels, but also offered the clinching proof of the wide disparity between the inner and outer worlds of Abraham Lincoln."[54] When Holland questioned Herndon about Lincoln's religious beliefs, Herndon snorted, *"The less said the better."* To which Holland winked and said, "O never mind, I'll fix that."[55]

Herndon was so incensed at what he believed was an outright lie by Holland and Bateman that he sought to investigate the matter himself. He cross-examined Bateman as he would a witness in court, although notes of these interviews have been lost. Bateman wrote a letter to Herndon a few years later, clearly annoyed with what he saw as badgering: "Mr Lincoln was deeply solemnly *religious*—it inspired me with awe . . . I had no thought of Orthodoxy or heterodoxy—unitarianism, trinitarianism or any other ism during the whole of our Conversation & I don't suppose or *believe he had*. The room was full of God & high truths & the awfulness of Coming Events. . . . He was alone with the Great God the problem of his Countrys future & his own & I but heard the Communings of his soul." Another biographer, Isaac Arnold, wrote to Bateman about the matter and then reported back to Herndon with disgust: "In regard to Mr Bateman he does not stand up very squarely. I wrote to him once to ask him if Holland had repeated him correctly & he replied—as I recollect 'substantially.'" The controversy was over the words, "Christ is God." Under cross-examination Bateman appears not to be able to swear to that all-important phrase.[56]

The most thorough analysis of the Holland-Herndon controversy has concluded, "The incident has a basis in fact. Neither Bateman nor Holland would have created such a story out of whole cloth. But Bateman was under very strong temptation to enlarge upon this incident, and had five years in which to magnify it in his

own mind. The then recent death of
Mr. Lincoln and the strong desire of
Christian people for a clear statement of his faith, made it easy to
color the recollection and sketch in
details."[57] Lincoln surely had the
conversation with Bateman about
the immorality of slavery, and the
anger Lincoln had toward pro-slavery ministers was real. He had no
patience with those who would try to
justify slavery on Biblical grounds. As
will be seen, he viewed those who

William H. Herndon. (*Lincoln
Museum*)

claimed that the Bible was a pro-slavery text as directly contradict-
ing the teachings of Jesus Christ. He wrote with great sarcasm in a
fragment of notes on the subject of slavery:

> The sum of pro-slavery theology seems to be this:
> "Slavery is not universally right, nor yet universally
> wrong; it is better for some people to be slaves; and, in
> such cases, it is the Will of God that they be such."
> Certainly there is no contending against the Will of
> God; but still there is some difficulty in ascertaining,
> and applying it, to particular cases. For instance we will
> suppose the Rev. Dr. Ross has a slave named Sambo,
> and the question is "Is it the Will of God that Sambo
> shall remain a slave, or be set free?" The Almighty gives
> no audable answer to the question, and his revelation—
> the Bible—gives none—or, at most, none but such as
> admits of a squabble, as to it's meaning. No one thinks
> of asking Sambo's opinion on it. So, at last, it comes to
> this, that Dr. Ross is to decide the question. And while

he consider[s] it, he sits in the shade, with gloves on his hands, and subsists on the bread that Sambo is earning in the burning sun. If he decides that God Wills Sambo to continue a slave, he thereby retains his own comfortable position; but if he decides that God will's Sambo to be free, he thereby has to walk out of the shade, throw off his gloves, and delve for his own bread. Will Dr. Ross be actuated by that perfect impartiality, which has ever been considered most favorable to correct decisions?[58]

Lincoln's dismay about the ministers in Springfield who supported pro-slavery candidates was real. The phrase "Christ is God" is most likely Bateman's unfortunate gloss to a story that was powerful enough on its own. As Barton observes, any biographer who adds that phrase to Lincoln's conversation with Bateman "does it at his own risk."[59]

THE ELECTION OF LINCOLN TO THE Presidency in November 1860 would change his religious thought even further. The crushing weight of responsibility as he left Springfield to assume his duties as chief executive caused his mind to once again wander toward the subjects of God and death. As he visited his stepmother for the last time, he finally saw the grave of his father. He asked that a stone be put up to mark it. His stepmother broke down during his visit. Herndon recounts, "The parting, when the good old woman, with tears streaming down her cheeks, gave him a mother's benediction, expressing the fear that his life might be taken by his enemies, will never be forgotten by those who witnessed it." When he visited the widow of an old friend from New Salem, she too told him that she feared for his life. He tried to calm her by joking, "Hannah, if they do kill me I shall never die again."[60]

The decade before he left on his momentous journey to the Presidency had been marked by tremendous growth in Lincoln's spirituality. One scholar has surmised, "The Lincoln of this period did indeed evince a new seriousness in tone and a sharper moral edge. This seems to have been related to a greater thoughtfulness about religion." He no longer was an infidel. In fact, he might be considered a Christian. However, one point remained that would stop many from defining him as thus. It was the one Bateman tried to supply by putting the words "Christ is God" in Lincoln's mouth. As Keyes, the Springfield tailor, recalls it, Lincoln told him, "As to christian theory, that, Christ is God, or equal to the Creator he said had better be taken for granted – for by the test of reason all might become infidels on that subject, for evidence of Christs divinity Came to us in somewhat doubtful Shape – but that the Sistom of Christianity was an ingenious one at least – and was Calculated to do good - ." Perhaps Lincoln's doubt on this particular article of faith was why Noyes Miner, the pastor of Springfield's First Baptist Church and Lincoln's friend, said Lincoln "was what is termed an experimental Christian."[61]

On the morning of February 11, 1861, Lincoln and a few companions rode in the drizzling rain from the hotel to the train waiting to take him to Washington. Lincoln greeted friends and well-wishers for some time before mounting the platform of the last car. Lincoln was so moved he could barely speak. He removed his hat, and with a quivering voice he told the crowd:

> My friends—No one, not in my situation, can appreciate my feeling of sadness at this parting. To this place, and the kindness of these people, I owe every thing. Here I have lived a quarter of a century, and have passed from a young to an old man. Here my children have been born, and one is buried. I now leave, not

knowing when, or whether ever, I may return, with a
task before me greater than that which rested upon
Washington. Without the assistance of that Divine
Being, who ever attended him, I cannot succeed. With
that assistance I cannot fail. Trusting in Him, who can
go with me, and remain with you and be every where
for good, let us confidently hope that all will yet be
well. To His care commending you, as I hope in your
prayers you will commend me, I bid you an affectionate farewell.

At the end of this address one witness reported that there was
"scarcely a dry eye in all that vast crowd." The train pulled away as
soon as Lincoln finished, and the crowd watched with their heads
uncovered as it moved out of sight.[62]

Chapter 4

EARLY CHRISTIAN SOURCES AND LINCOLN'S RHETORIC

He says I have a proneness for quoting scripture.
—*Abraham Lincoln, speech in Springfield, Illinois, July 17, 1858*

WHILE LINCOLN WAS PRESIDENT, he "offered up prayers and supplications" to God. He often went to the Bible and meditated on its meaning and, as will be seen, at one point looked for a sign from God to issue the Emancipation Proclamation. Lincoln had to look no further than the New Testament to see Christ's own example of prayer and humility. From anecdotal evidence and through his own words, Lincoln's view of Jesus was surprisingly close to the view of his earliest followers. In fact, the irony is that many of the pious nineteenth-century people who would call Lincoln an infidel themselves believe in concepts that were alien to the first- and second-generation Christians.

Lincoln was not the first President to hold unconventional views on Christianity. Thomas Jefferson made his own version of the Gospels by cutting out the parts he didn't like and pasting those he did in a book, "Morals of Jesus." Jefferson, who had no shortage of self-confidence, said he could tell "the matter which is evidently his, and which is as easily distinguishable as diamonds in a dunghill." Not surprisingly, the Jesus that emerged was remarkably a lot like Thomas Jefferson, a liberal interested in human progress who disliked religious orthodoxy and clergymen.[1]

Jesus is known as a wise man or teacher and as a miracle worker in the Gospels and in a brief first-century mention of him by the Jewish historian Flavius Josephus. This point would have been especially important to Lincoln who, as will be seen, admired the moral teachings of Jesus greatly.[2]

Another aspect of Jesus of Nazareth may have appealed to Lincoln. "In the eyes of most classical authors Jesus would likely be, in a word, a *troublemaker*."[3] Lincoln may have appreciated Jesus' unsettling pronouncements to those in power because he himself was enough of a "troublemaker" that his first election precipitated the breakup of the Union. Just as Jesus once said, "Think not that I am come to send peace on earth: I came not to send peace, but a sword" (Matthew 10:34) as he proceeded to cleanse the Temple, Lincoln warned his followers not to relent on the issue of slavery expansion when the South was threatening to secede. He wrote an Illinois Senator, "Have none of it. Stand firm. The tug has to come, & the better now, than any time hereafter."[4]

THE FOUR CANONICAL GOSPELS were written roughly in a twenty-five-year period from 65 to 90 C.E. Mark was written first shortly before the destruction of the Jewish Temple by the Romans in 70 C.E. Both Luke and Matthew wrote about 80 C.E., and John wrote last, around 90 C.E. These dates are approximate but reflect the wide consensus of scholars, both secular and Christian. The names given to the gospels were added during the second century. There is no reason to presume that the writer of John was really one of the twelve, John, son of Zebedee, but it is convenient to refer to the evangelists by the name their gospels bear.[5]

The Gospel of John, written later than Mark, Matthew, and Luke, is different from the others in tone and in the story it tells. Probably composed independent of the others, it contains a Jesus that is the "Word" made flesh. It is more philosophical and poetic than the others. Jesus in John's Gospel makes the famous so-called "I" statements. "I am the living bread that came down from heaven" (John 6:51) or "I am the good shepherd: the good shepherd giveth his life for the sheep" (John 10:11). Most famous of these is "I am the way, the truth, and the life; no man cometh unto the Father, but by me" (John 14:6). These words seem to reflect the early church's view of Jesus' status rather than what he may have actually said. As John Meier states, "The Johannine presentation of Jesus' ministry is just too massively different to be derived from the Synoptics; and even where John does parallel the Synoptics, the strange mixture and erratic pattern is best explained by a stream of tradition similar to, but independent of, the Synoptics."[6]

Significantly, Lincoln shied away from quoting John. While John has some of the most beautiful language in the New Testament, Lincoln may have been uncomfortable with its presentation of Jesus as being fully aware of his divine nature. The Word made flesh was not something Lincoln could accept. He preferred the more "human" nature of Jesus as presented in the Synoptics.

The first three Gospels, Matthew, Mark, and Luke, are called the Synoptic Gospels because they all tell essentially the same story, or synopsis. The so-called "Synoptic problem" refers to the relationship among these three texts, since there is much shared material among them. (The British Christian apologist G. K. Chesterton could have been referring to this quandary when he said, "The Christian ideal has not been tried and found wanting; it has been found difficult and left untried." Nowhere is the Christian ideal as difficult as in the Q source for the Gospels of Matthew and Luke.)[7] The most common explanation of the relationship between the three is the two-source solution. It is based on the idea that Mark, the simplest and shortest Gospel, was written first. The evangelists Matthew and Luke then used Mark as a source for their gospels. They also used material now lost to us, a hypothetical source referred to as Q, for the German word *Quelle* ("source"), a theory first advanced almost two hundred years ago in Germany.

New Testament scholar Marcus Borg writes why the hypothetical source is so widely accepted today: "The basis for the 'Q hypothesis' . . . is a large amount of material (over two hundred verses) found in both Matthew and Luke, but not in Mark. Most scholars do not think that either the author of Matthew or the author of Luke knew the other's Gospel. Therefore the material they share in common cannot be the result of one borrowing from the other, but must come from an earlier written source to which they both had access." There are just too many differences in telling and material peculiar to themselves to believe Matthew and Luke were aware of each other's writing. Borg admits that the Q document is hypothetical and that it has never been found. He writes, "It is therefore possible to deny that it existed, and some scholars do not accept the Q hypothesis. But most do. My impression is that at least 90 percent of contemporary Gospel scholars do. It seems to them (and to me) a necessary hypothesis."[8]

The Q source is for the most part a collection of the sayings of Jesus, with a few bits of narrative material. There are no birth or passion narratives, and only one miracle story. Most of Jesus' famous sayings, such as the Sermon on the Mount, and many of his moral teachings are present in it. Q was supposedly put in its final form about 50 C.E., in time for its incorporation into Matthew and Luke. Lincoln, as it will be seen, had a special fondness for the Q material whenever he quoted the gospels.[9]

All four Gospels date the beginning of Jesus' ministry with his baptism from John the Baptist. John was a prophet known for his baptism ritual that symbolized the purity required to be in God's favor. This has an excellent chance of being a true historical event because early Christians would not have invented something that could cause them embarrassment. These events are so well known that the believers had to deal with them rather than cover them up.[10]

Applying this to Jesus' baptism, Meier states, "There is no credible reason why the early church of the first generation should have gone out of its way to invent a story that would only create enormous difficulties for its inventor. After all, the story of baptism presents the church's Lord being put in a position of inferiority to John by accepting from him a baptism of repentance for the forgiveness of sins."[11]

All of this raises the puzzling question of Lincoln's own lack of baptism. Some thought Lincoln would have been baptized had he not been assassinated, as the last part of his life was the most religious. The fact remains that he was not baptized. The most obvious answer to that may be that being baptized implied membership in whatever sect baptized him. Lincoln was too honest to join a sect whose dogma he could not wholeheartedly endorse.

If Jesus himself did experience an awakening of spirituality by John and his baptism ritual, what was it about John's message that appealed to him? John was a fiery eschatological prophet who preached God's imminent judgment. According to the Q material, John preached God's coming judgment on Israel (Matthew 3:7-12/Luke 3:7-9). John's popularity among the Jewish people would lead to his downfall. In politically tense first-century Palestine, a man who got large crowds could be dangerous to the powers that be, and Herod Antipas put him to death. Jesus may have well seen his own fate foreshadowed in John's.[12]

Just as John the Baptist's message appealed to Jesus, it also would have appealed to Lincoln. According to a previously quoted letter by Lincoln's friend Isaac Cogdal, Lincoln thought the preaching of divine punishment would be beneficial. Cogdal stated, "And he added this remark, that punishment being a provision of the gospel system, he was not sure but the world would be better off if a little more punishment was preached by our ministers, and not so much pardon for sin." Lincoln also once approvingly quoted from Thomas Jefferson on the subject of America and slavery, when stating, "I tremble for my country when I remember God is just." Lincoln could think of "Holy Willie" in Burns's poem as an example of what happens when grace and election are preached without the fire and brimstone of John and the historical Jesus.[13]

Lincoln, like John the Baptist, had no sympathy with the defense of religious status. John thought the Jews could not claim anything special since God could create "children unto Abraham" (Matthew 3:9) from the rocks. Likewise, later in the Civil War, Lincoln had no sympathy when two women with Confederate husbands argued for their release on the grounds that they were "religious." Lincoln was so angered by this that he wrote an account to be printed in the newspapers, "The President's Last, Shortest, and Best Speech":

> On thursday of last week two ladies from Tennessee came before the President asking the release of their husbands held as prisoners of war at Johnson's Island. . . . At each of the interviews one of the ladies urged that her husband was a religious man. On saturday the President ordered the release of the prisoners, and then said to this lady "You say your husband is a religious man; tell him when you meet him, that I say I am not

much of a judge of religion, but that, in my opinion, the religion that sets men to rebel and fight against their government, because, as they think, that government does not sufficiently help some men to eat their bread on the sweat of other men's faces, is not the sort of religion upon which people can get to heaven!"[14]

The essence of the Gospel of Jesus could be found in "seek ye first the kingdom of God and his righteousness" (Matthew 6:33). The words "Kingdom of God" and "Kingdom of Heaven" are favorites of Jesus and appear 105 times in the Synoptics. There is only one clear example of Lincoln using it, on his son Eddie's tombstone. But what does the phrase mean? Jesus scholar E. P. Sanders writes, "There are, however, two meanings that would have been more or less self-evident given standard Jewish views. One is that God reigns in heaven; the 'kingdom of God' or 'kingdom of heaven' exists eternally there. God occasionally acts in history, but he completely and consistently governs only heaven. The second is that in the future God will rule the earth. . . . Briefly put: the kingdom of God always exists *there*; in the *future* it will exist *here*." At the very least then, the Kingdom of God requires God's intervention in human affairs. In short, a new order will be born.[15]

The Beatitudes, a series of blessings so named from the Latin word for happiness, in Q (Matthew 5:3-12/Luke 6:20-23) give a hint of how different God's kingdom will be compared to earthly existence. The Beatitudes differ in Matthew and Luke, but a core would likely be the phrases: "Happy are the poor for theirs is the kingdom of heaven. Happy are the mourners for they shall be comforted. Happy are the hungry for they shall be satisfied." Here those that are suffering will be comforted. In Luke there are also the lesser quoted woes. It is hard to say whether they are originally part of Q since they are not in Matthew. After the positive reversals, Luke has Jesus say, "But woe unto you that are rich! For ye have received your consolation. Woe unto you that are full! For ye shall hunger. Woe unto you that laugh now! For ye shall mourn and weep. Woe unto you, when all men shall speak well of you! For so did their fathers to the false prophets" (Luke 6:24-26). Whether this is Luke's redaction of Q or an invention, it shows the Kingdom of God as a reversal of present circumstances.[16]

Lincoln never directly quoted these lines of Luke, but it appears he approved of the notion of the powerful brought low. In a note he made about slavery in 1854, he uses the theme of reversal:

> If A. can prove, however conclusively, that he may, of right, enslave B.—why may not B. snatch the same argument, and prove equally, that he may enslave A?—You say A. is white, and B. is black. It is color, then; the lighter, having the right to enslave the darker? Take care. By this rule, you are to be slave to the first man you meet, with a fairer skin than your own. You do not mean color exactly?—You mean the whites are intellectually the superiors of the blacks, and, therefore have the right to enslave them? Take care again. By this rule, you are to be slave to the first man you meet, with an intellect superior to your own. But, say you, it is a question of interest; and, if you can make it your interest, you have the right to enslave another. Very well. And if he can make it his interest, he has the right to enslave you.[17]

In Lincoln's mind the slaveholder and his ideology were not welcome in the Kingdom of God.

It is the broad consensus that Jesus spoke of the Kingdom of God or Heaven, but debate has centered on whether Jesus meant it to be a forthcoming event, or the present that could be brought about by the actions of the God's people. The weight of the testimony is Jesus' view, like John's, was *eschatological*. He saw that God would intervene shortly to bring about his kingdom.

The best known example of this is the Lord's Prayer. Lincoln would have heard it many times in his life, especially when he attended church. Boiling down the two versions (Matthew 6:9-13/Luke 11:2-4) to the probable Q form produces the following:

Father,

hallowed be your name.

Your Kingdom come.

Our daily bread give us today.

And forgive us our debts

As we forgive our debtors.

And do not lead us to the test.

Since the kingdom must "come," it is not here yet.[18]

Jesus' message, however, was not a simple repetition of John the Baptist's. According to Meier, "Drawing some disciples from this group [John's], Jesus soon struck out on his own with a new message of God's imminent yet present kingdom, a message addressed to all of Israel." The Kingdom of Heaven was already present within the ministry of Jesus. His healings and fellowship with sinners were evidence of God's Kingdom breaking through into this world.[19]

The clearest expression of this is Jesus' answer to John the Baptist's question in Q. The tradition states, "Now, when John had heard in the prison the works of Christ, he sent two of his disciples, And said unto him, Art thou he that should come, or do we look for another? Jesus answered and said unto them, Go and show John again those things which ye do hear and see: The blind receive their sight, and the lame walk, the lepers are cleansed, and the deaf hear, the dead are raised up, and the poor have the gospel preached to them" (Matthew 11:2-5/Luke 7:19-22).

Q also contains this blessing of Jesus to his disciples, "But blessed *are* your eyes, for they see; and your ears, for they hear. For verily I say unto you that many prophets and righteous *men* have desired to see *those things* which ye see, and have not seen *them*; and to hear *those things* which ye hear, and have not heard *them*" (Matthew 13:16-17/Luke 10:23-14). Here is Jesus saying that his actions are bringing forth a new world.

The Gospel of Luke also has some material speaking of the Kingdom as present. At one point, Jesus exorcises a demon and says, "But if I, with the finger of God, cast out demons, no doubt the kingdom of God is come upon you" (Luke 11:20). At another point, Jesus answers the Pharisees' question about the Kingdom: "And when he was demanded of the Pharisees, when the kingdom of God should come, he answered them and said, The kingdom of God cometh not with observation. Neither shall they say, Lo here! Or, lo there! For, behold, the kingdom of God is in the midst of you" (Luke 17:20-21).

Horsely and Silberman, two scholars of early Christianity, have also pointed out this nuance of the Gospels. Speaking of the scholars who wrote of Jesus' eschatological views, they write, "And they believed that Jesus, when placed in proper historical context in the traditions of second-temple Judaism, should not be understood as a mild-mannered teacher and healer but an uncompromising prophet of doom and destruction who really believed that the world as he and other members of his generation knew it was about to pass away." However, they also recognize, "it is hard to reconcile that grim understanding with the joyful, life-affirming message that the former carpenter from Nazareth announced in the people's midst. . . . In both John's and Jesus' preaching, the coming of the Kingdom of God meant a revolution in the way people behaved toward each other and their recognition that they should have no Caesars, tetrarchs, centurions, or overlords above them except for the one God."

Ultimately it is not an either/or, when it comes to eschatological or non-eschatological message for Jesus. It is both. However, the work of God must bring this Kingdom about.[20]

Lincoln had his own version of what a "Kingdom of God" could be like on earth. The closing lines of his Second Inaugural Address, carved on the walls of the Lincoln Memorial, read, "With malice toward none; with charity for all; with firmness in the right, as God gives us to see the right, let us strive on to finish the work we are in; to bind up the nation's wounds; to care for him who shall have borne the battle, and for his widow, and his orphan—to do all which may achieve and cherish a just, and a lasting peace, among ourselves, and with all nations."[21]

Lincoln would not have subscribed to all of the New Testament. He was not one to believe in miracles in the traditional sense of the word. After his third son, Willie, died, Mary Todd Lincoln went to séances to find comfort and believed in the signs that they provided. Lincoln sometimes attended for entertainment and, more important, to protect his wife from charlatans. When the spiritualist Lord Colchester produced clicking sounds seemingly out of nowhere, Lincoln asked the head of the Smithsonian Institution, Joseph Henry, to investigate. When he found the sounds were made from a device attached to Colchester's arm, Lincoln was relieved to learn how it was done. This is not to say that Lincoln held Colchester and Jesus on the same level. We have no evidence about how Lincoln viewed Jesus' miracles, but this does show that Lincoln was not sympathetic to things that went against the laws of nature.[22]

THE LAST SUPPER IS RECORDED IN all four gospels and had such an effect on Jesus' followers that a ritual commemorating it was created shortly after his death. Paul writes to the Corinthians, "that the

Lord Jesus, the *same* night in which he was betrayed, took bread; And when he had given thanks, he broke it, and said, Take, eat; this is my body, which is broken for you: this do in remembrance of me. After the same manner also *he took* the cup, when he had supped, saying, This cup is the new testament in my blood: this do, as often as ye drink *it*, in remembrance of me" (1 Corinthians 11:23-25).[23] Lincoln would have heard these last words whenever he took communion while attending church.

Jesus' death on the cross is the most sure and verifiable fact about him, and the cross has become the symbol of the entire religion. Indeed the first time a Roman historian mentions Jesus, in 115 C.E., it is to say that Jesus "suffered the extreme penalty during the reign of Tiberius at the hands of one of our procurators, Pontius Pilatus." Upon entering Jerusalem for the final time, Jesus "cleansed" the temple. He was arrested a few days later by Temple authorities and turned over to Pilate to be put to death. He died on the Friday of Passover and was buried. This is a simplification of the facts, yet it is the bare-bones narrative in the Synoptics. The fact that the authorities went after Jesus alone seems to indicate they didn't think his followers were especially troubling. Also, there was no better inducement for the Passover crowds to behave themselves than a public and brutal crucifixion.[24]

The death of Jesus was a shock to his disciples, and would have ended any Jesus movement had it not been for the experience that some of his followers had three days later. There are two distinct narratives of the Resurrection: the women at the empty tomb and the appearances to the disciples. It is hard to reconcile the chronology in the various gospels.[25]

Religious scholars have taken to task those who believe what happened is obvious. One writes, "The reader who thinks that it is all perfectly clear—the physical, historical Jesus got up and walked around—should study Luke and Paul more carefully. The disciples could not recognize him; he was not 'flesh and blood' but a 'spiritual body.'" Meier also takes issue with those who think it is clear. In making a point about the nature of the resurrection, he states, "The fundamentalists would almost have a rather crass resurrection view. Most traditional Christians have at least read Paul, First Corinthians 15 about the necessary transformation, as well as the Resurrection appearance narratives in the Gospels. They think in terms of transformation as well as continuity."[26]

The historian cannot of course "prove" the Resurrection happened. What can be proven is that Jesus' followers *believed* he had risen from the dead. Many rationalist explanations for the Resurrection include mass hallucination and deceit by select disciples, but there is no doubt of the sincerity of the early Christian belief. The evidence from Paul and his letters in the first Christian generation is that this was the significant event for which Christ was to be remembered. Without the Resurrection there is no Christian faith. As Paul states, "And if Christ be not risen, then *is* our preaching vain, and your faith *is* also vain" (1 Corinthians 15:14).

Lincoln made no specific comment on the nature of the resurrection. Rev. James Smith's arguments about the witnesses to it would have fit his lawyerly sensibilities, but Lincoln did not make his views known on the subject. After all, according to Paul, belief in the resurrection was definitely the earliest Christian tenet. The question of an empty tomb may not have bothered him, since, to Paul, the appearances to the disciples were what mattered.

The only books in the New Testament that can be said to go back to the first Christian generation are the seven undisputed Pauline letters (Romans, 1 and 2 Corinthians, Galatians, Philippians, 1 Thessalonians, and Philemon). The other letters attributed to Paul are thought to have been written later by others in Paul's name. The seven undisputed epistles were written from 50 to 58 C.E. during Paul's missionary activity. As one scholar once put it, because Paul's message centered on the death and resurrection of Jesus, he was not that interested in what Jesus said or did during his ministry. One German student of Paul concluded, "The Jesus of history is apparently dismissed. Paul himself never met him. And, as he himself asserts in debates with opponents who obviously based their case on the fact that they had known Jesus, even if Paul did not know Christ from the human point of view, he regarded him thus no longer (2 Corinthians. 5:16)." Paul's lack of commentary on the teachings of Jesus probably account for Lincoln's general silence on Paul in his religious utterances.[27]

Paul's assignment of the chief blame of Christ's death to his fellow Jews has led to the suffering of generations of Jews as "Christ-killers." In the earliest surviving Christian document, written twenty years after the crucifixion to the Church in Thessalonica, Paul says, "for ye also have suffered like things of your own countrymen, even as they *have* of the Jews, Who both killed the Lord Jesus and their own prophets, and have persecuted us; and they please not God, and are contrary to all men, Forbidding us to speak to the Gentiles that they might be saved, to fill up their sins always; for the wrath is come upon them to the uttermost" (1 Thessalonians 2:14-16).[28]

It is of note that Lincoln himself never indulged in the anti-Semitism that many others of his day did. When General Grant had "Jews, as a class" expelled from his military department for what he saw as dishonest business dealings with his troops, the Attorney General thought it was a matter of no importance. Lincoln would have none of this and had General Henry W. Halleck write Grant that Grant could expel traders in his department, "but as it in terms prescribed an entire religious class, some of whom are fighting in our ranks, the President deemed it necessary to revoke it." Lincoln also pushed Congress to pass a law to have Jews as chaplains in the regiments with Jewish members.[29]

It is important to know how the status of Christ changed in the years immediately following the Resurrection. By the fourth century orthodox Christianity became formalized, and "heresies" such as Arianism, which held that since Jesus Christ was human, he must have been created by God and was thus inferior to God, were stamped out. Gnosticism, which held that Christ was not truly human and not of this world, was also crushed. Orthodox Christianity as represented in the Council of Nicaea said that Christ had to have been of "the same substance" of God. This was represented in the Nicene Creed, which is still recited as the core belief of many Christian denominations. It reads:

> We believe in one God the Father All-Sovereign
> Maker of all things visible and invisible
> And in one Lord Jesus Christ
> The Son of God
> begotten of the Father
> only begotten
> that is
> of the substance of the Father
> God of God
> Light of Light
> true God of true God
> begotten not made
> of one substance with the Father.

The statements in the Nicene Creed have been the foundation of Christianity since 325 C.E., making them the yardstick by which Lincoln's Christianity has been measured.[30]

Is it fair to measure Lincoln's adherence to Christianity by that measure, or by what Christians believed in the earliest days following the crucifixion? By the former measure Lincoln would most likely be classified as a non-Christian, but what about the latter? In the late first century, *proto-orthodox* beliefs were the belief of the early Christians that ultimately evolved into what we today know as Christianity. What did these earliest Christians believe? It is possible Lincoln was more in step with their beliefs.

To find the earliest beliefs, one must turn to the earliest writings, those of Paul. Within the Pauline corpus are preserved some early Christian formulas which go back to the time right after the Resurrection. As stated above, the evidence can be maddeningly ambiguous on key areas of belief, but it is possible to make some reasonable deductions.

The earliest surviving Christian formula is found in Paul's first letter to the Corinthians. Paul must have heard this formula immediately after converting which was no more than three years after Christ's crucifixion. Paul had been persecuting the new sect as being heretical Jews when he had his Damascus road experience, and must have been taught by the very people he had been seeking to punish shortly before. Paul wrote to the Christians in Corinth about twenty years afterwards, regarding the Resurrection of the dead. He recalls an old statement of faith. It reads:

> Moreover, brethren, I declare unto you the gospel which I preached unto you, which also ye have received, and in which ye stand; By which also ye are saved, if ye keep in memory what I preached unto you, unless ye have believed in vain. For I delivered unto you first of all that which I also received, that Christ died for our sins according to the scriptures; And that he was buried, and that he rose again the third day according to the scriptures; And that he was seen of Cephas (Peter), then of the twelve. After that, he was

seen of above five hundred brethren at once, of whom
the greater part remain unto this present time, but
some are fallen asleep. After that, he was seen of James;
then, of all the apostles. (1 Corinthians 15:1-7)[31]

The phrase "according to the scriptures" is intriguing because
it shows that the early Christians almost immediately turned to the
Old Testament for guidance in trying to understand what happened. For example, the twenty-second Psalm in particular was
very valuable to them: "My God, my God, why hast thou forsaken
me?" (Psalms 22:1). These are Jesus' last words in Mark and
Matthew. Also this passage helped shape the Passion narratives:
"For dogs have compassed me; the assembly of the wicked have
enclosed me; they have pierced my hands and my feet. I may
count all my bones; they look *and* stare upon me. They part my
garments among them, and cast lots upon my vesture" (Psalms
22:16-18).

Interestingly enough, Lincoln also used a passage from the
Psalms to illustrate his own behavior. When on his way to
Washington for his first inaugural in 1861, Lincoln stopped at
Independence Hall in Philadelphia. He said, "All my political war-
fare has been in favor of the teachings coming forth from that
sacred hall. May my right hand forget its cunning and my tongue
cleave to the roof of my mouth, if I ever prove false to those teachings." He had paraphrased the famous lines "If I forget thee, O
Jerusalem, let my right hand forget *her cunning*. If I do not remember thee, let my tongue cleave to the roof of my mouth, if I prefer
not Jerusalem above my chief joy" (Psalms 137:5-6).[32]

Another section in scripture immediately attracted Christian
attention in helping them understand Christ's passion. It was the
"suffering servant" of Isaiah. It must have caught Christian attention because it seemed to explain the reasons for Christ's death.

One passage reads, "But he *was* wounded for our transgressions, *he was* bruised for our iniquities; the chastisement for our peace *was* upon him, and with his stripes we are healed. All we like sheep have gone astray; we have turned every one to is own way, and the Lord hath laid on him the iniquity of us all" (Isaiah 53:5-6). Early on Christ's death was seen as atonement for the sins of all. It wasn't a tragedy or an injustice; it was a sign of God's love. This was incorporated in a formula along with Christ's Resurrection and appearances. This was a doctrine Lincoln could accept because as he once told Cogdal, "all that was lost by the transgression of Adam was made good by the atonement, all that was lost by the fall was made good by the sacrifice."[33]

While Lincoln shied away from quoting Paul, he agreed in general with Paul's conception of Christ. Lincoln gave much more emphasis on the wisdom of the earthly Jesus' sayings than Paul did. One should not make too much of the differences between them. Lincoln did not view Jesus as simply a teacher or sage. He agreed with Paul on the atonement. They both saw Christ's death as saving for humankind, which is under indictment from God for their sinful actions.

To Paul and the early Christians Jesus was Lord and also an expression of God's wisdom and spirit. One scholar of Paul has concluded, "Paul saw the human Jesus as the revelation of the one God. It mattered to him that this human being Jesus *remained* human, now that he was enthroned as the Lord of the world." If Jesus is an example of God's spirit, it is not necessarily a description that puts Jesus as part of God. The inevitable tension between a monotheistic view and an exalted picture of Jesus has been impossible for some to reconcile. Many Christian theologians have found the idea that Christ was God in the New Testament, but Lincoln's reading of the Bible did not find it necessary or self-evident. He said as much to a Springfield tailor when he said, "evidence of Christ's divinity came to us in somewhat doubtful Shape."[34]

One religious scholar has commented on the controversy this problem created for the early church and its implications for its later beliefs. He writes, "As early Christianity developed, the post-Easter Jesus increasingly functioned as a divine reality within the community. Even before the gospels were written, prayers were addressed to Jesus as if to God, and hymns praised Jesus as divine. By early second century, Ignatius could speak of 'our God, Jesus Christ.'" This caused a serious problem. The question and answer can be put as the scholar states, "How could early Christians reconcile their experience and devotion to the post-Easter Jesus as a divine reality with their commitment to monotheism? The solution to the conundrum was ultimately the Trinity, expressed in the trinitarian pattern of the Nicene Creed."[35] The Christians of the frontier in Lincoln's time were far removed from the religious world of Paul, and were living with the Nicene Creed. It is possible that they would have thought even Paul, let alone Lincoln, un-Christian in his beliefs![36]

Lincoln appears to have stayed with his monotheistic view, and was unable to accept the Trinity as a fact. He refers to God and no other divine figure in his speeches. Perhaps the he could not reconcile the doctrine of the Trinity with logic and reason, and simply repeating religious dogma for its own sake would have been against his nature.

FOR LINCOLN, THE FIRST-CENTURY eschatological prophet who taught, healed, and referred to himself as the "Son of man" was a "savior." Lincoln saw Jesus' teachings as being wise and referred to them often. He even saw in Jesus' death atonement for sins. Lincoln was not against the doctrine of punishment as God's work, though he saw it as a chastisement and a lesson rather than as punishment for its own sake. In short, there is much in the Jesus tradition and proto-orthodox belief that Lincoln believed in.[37]

The knowledge of Jesus and early Christianity gained by historians over the years helps to elucidate the nature of Lincoln's beliefs. Wayne Temple concludes that Lincoln was a "monotheist" but cannot go further. Like others he shies away from calling Lincoln a "Christian." Perhaps Temple is right in not wanting to call Lincoln a Christian in the orthodox sense. However, Lincoln can be called a Christian if judged by the pre-Nicene stages of the faith. Lincoln was indeed a proto-orthodox Christian and close to the earliest beliefs of the Christian faith.[38] The strongest evidence for this view can be found in Lincoln's own rhetorical use of the Synoptic Gospels.

No evidence exists that Lincoln knew about the Synoptic-problem or Q (which had been postulated by his time), but when quoting the New Testament, he seems partial toward its passages. Herndon said of Lincoln, "His forte and power lay in digging out for himself and securing for his mind its own food, to be assimilated unto himself." Lincoln could reason down to what were probably the original words of Jesus when studying the gospels. What is so startling about this is that it puts Lincoln very close to the teachings of the historical Jesus and early Christianity.[39]

The first recoverable use of Q by Lincoln is an oblique reference in a speech on temperance in 1842. Lincoln supported a temperance group, the Washingtonians, because they did not just condemn drunkards but tried to reform them through example and persuasion. He stated approvingly, "*They* (Washingtonians) adopt a more enlarged philanthropy. *They* go for present as well as future good. *They* labor for all *now* living, as well as all *hereafter* to live. *They* teach *hope* to all—*despair* to none. As applying to *their* cause, *they* deny the doctrine of unpardonable sin. As in

Christianity it is taught, so in this *they* teach, that 'While the lamp holds out to burn, The vilest sinner may return.'" Lincoln's reference to the "unpardonable sin" is an allusion to Jesus saying only one sin is truly beyond forgiveness: "And whosoever speaketh a word against the Son of man, it shall be forgiven him; but whosoever speaketh *against* the Holy Spirit, it shall not be forgiven him, neither in this age, neither in the *age* to come" (Matthew 12:32/Luke 12:10).[40]

The first clear instance of Lincoln using Q material comes in an 1848 letter about the Mexican War to a Baptist minister. Congressman Lincoln was upset with the minister's justification of the Polk administration's conduct of the Mexican War. Lincoln thought the United States was being unjust to its weaker southern neighbor. In reference to what he perceived as provocations by Polk toward Mexico before the war, Lincoln wrote, "Possibly you consider those acts too small for notice. Would you venture to so consider them, had they been committed by any nation on earth, against the humblest of our people? I know you would not. Then I ask, is the precept 'Whatsoever ye would that men should do to you, do ye even so to them' obsolete? — of no force? — of no application?" Lincoln saw Christ's wisdom applicable not just to individuals but to nations as well.[41]

Here was the famous Golden Rule. In Q, Jesus told the crowds, "Therefore, all things whatsoever ye would that men should do to you, do ye even so to them; for this is the law and the prophets" (Matthew 7:12/Luke 6:31). Lincoln found this to be a wise guide for human behavior. As President Lincoln would tell a friend about the Bible, "It is a good book for us to obey — it contains the ten commandments, the golden rule, and many other rules which ought to be followed. No man was ever the worst for living according to the directions of the Bible." Lincoln would use the Golden Rule again as President in reply to a delegation of clergy in 1864.

Speaking of pro-slavery theologians he said, "When, a year or two ago, those professedly holy men of the South, met in the semblance of prayer and devotion, and, in the name of Him who said 'As ye would all men should do unto you, do ye even so unto them' appealed to the christian world to aid them in doing to a whole race of men, as they would have no man do unto themselves." Lincoln quoted the version in Luke this time, something he generally didn't do. Like most people, he favored the use of Matthew's gospel. The simpler version in Luke must have appealed to him in this setting.[42]

Lincoln scholar Henry Jaffa sees the Golden Rule in a scrap written by Lincoln on slavery and democracy. Jaffa writes of Lincoln, "he constantly appealed to the Bible . . . as a source of moral authority, and never more so than when he said, 'As I would not be a *slave*, so I would not be a *master*. This expresses my idea of democracy. Whatever differs from this, to the extent of the difference is not democracy.' The first sentence is clearly an application of that Golden Rule that, according to Jesus, was the sum of the law and the prophets."[43]

Lincoln used Q again in an 1851 letter to his stepbrother about his dying father. Lincoln told Johnston to pass on to Thomas Lincoln a comforting message. He wrote, "I sincerely hope Father may yet recover his health; but at all events tell him to remember to call upon, and confide in, our great, and good, and merciful Maker; who will not turn away from him in any extremity. He notes the fall of a sparrow, and numbers the hairs of our heads; and He will not forget the dying man, who puts his trust in Him." The quoted part of the letter parallels Jesus' message to his disciples about the costs and benefits of discipleship. After telling them what evils may happen to them, Jesus also tells his disciples that God will look after them. In Q, Jesus states, "Are not two sparrows sold for a farthing? And one of them shall not fall on the ground without your Father. But the very hairs of your head are all numbered" (Matthew 10:29-30/Luke 12:6-7).[44]

Lincoln was remembered using passages recalling Q in court. In defending the law profession against a dishonest lawyer who had used information improperly from the other side of a case, Lincoln suppos-edly said, "The Wisest has said that 'no man can serve two masters.'" Here Lincoln quoted the Q verse, "No man can serve two masters: for either he will hate the one, and love the other; or else he will hold to the

Abraham Lincoln in 1858, two weeks before the final debate with Stephen A. Douglas. (*Library of Congress*)

one, and despise the other. Ye cannot serve God and mammon" (Matthew 6:24/Luke 16:13).[45]

In his famous debates with Stephen A. Douglas, Lincoln was more at home using scripture due to his Whig roots. The Whigs advocated moral reform of the nation and often used biblical lan-guage. Douglas was a Democrat whose political idol, Andrew Jackson, once refused to proclaim a fast day because he thought it violated the separation of church and state. In the debate with Douglas, the issue of slavery gave Lincoln the opportunity to use Q material. Douglas was so needled by this and, having no answer, even went against his Democratic inclinations and started to quote scripture back at Lincoln.[46]

In a speech in Chicago concerning the extension of slavery in 1858, Lincoln looked to Q to make a point against Stephen Douglas. Lincoln realized the country was not living up to the promises of the Declaration of Independence, so he gave a Biblical parallel:

My friend has said to me that I am a poor hand to quote Scripture. I will try it again, however. It is said in one of the admonitions of the Lord, "As your Father in Heaven is perfect, be ye also perfect." The Savior, I suppose, did not expect that any human creature could be perfect as the Father in Heaven; but He said, "As your Father in Heaven is perfect, be ye also perfect." He set that up as a standard, and he who did most towards reaching that standard, attained the highest degree of moral perfection. So I say in relation to the principle that all men are created equal, let it be as nearly reached as we can.

The Q verse quoted is "Be ye, therefore, perfect, even as your Father, who is in heaven, is perfect" (Matthew 5:48/Luke 6:36).[47]

Lincoln quoted the parable in Q about the lost sheep twice, first in relation to Stephen Douglas's fight with the Buchanan administration over the pro-slavery Lecompton Constitution in Kansas in 1858. The proposed Constitution was not popular sovereignty, which was Douglas's doctrine, so he opposed it. This won him some praise from Republicans in Illinois. In a speech in Springfield, Lincoln said:

He says I have a proneness for quoting scripture. If I should do so now, it occurs that perhaps he places himself somewhat upon the ground of the parable of the lost sheep which went astray upon the mountains, and when the owner of the hundred sheep found the one that was lost, and threw it upon his shoulders, and came home rejoicing, it was said that there was more rejoicing over the one sheep that was lost and had been found, than over the ninety and nine in the fold. The application is made by the Saviour in this parable, thus, "Verily, I say unto you, there is more rejoicing in heav-

en over one sinner that repenteth, than over ninety and
nine just persons that need no repentance."[48]

Lincoln used the parable again in reply to a New York delegation which had come to him to call on him in early 1861. He
spoke of the newly seceded states: "As towards the disaffected portion of our fellow-citizens, I will say, as every good man throughout the country must feel, that there will be more rejoicing over
one sheep that is lost, and is found, than over the ninety-and-nine
which have gone not astray." The Q version has Jesus comparing
God's care of his people to a shepherd and his concern of his flock.
Jesus tells his disciples:

> For the Son of man is come to save that which was lost.
> How think ye? If a man have an hundred sheep, and
> one of them be gone astray, doth he not leave the nine-
> ty and nine, and goeth into the mountains, and seeketh
> that which is gone astray? And if so be that he find it,
> verily I say unto you, he rejoiceth more over that sheep
> than over the ninety and nine which went not astray.
> Even so it is not the will of your Father, who is in heav-
> en, that one of these little ones should perish. (Matthew
> 18:11-14/Luke 15:4-7)[49]

In the fall of 1858 Lincoln wrote a fragment on pro-slavery theology, a topic for which he had no patience. Here he takes at their
word the claims of pro-slavery speakers and writers, who said that
slaves needed to be enslaved due to their supposed inferior abili-
ties, but then shows why this principle goes against the teachings
of Jesus. Lincoln wrote, "Suppose it is true, that the negro is inferior to the white, in the gifts of nature; is it not the exact reverse justice that the white should, for that reason, take from the negro, any
part of the little which has been given him? 'Give to him that is

needy' is the christian rule of charity; but 'Take from him that is needy' is the rule of slavery." Lincoln could find this aphorism from Q in the Gospel of Luke, "Give to every man that asketh of thee; and of him that taketh away thy goods ask *them* not again" (Luke 6:30/Matthew 6:1-4).[50]

Something about Douglas brought out quoting Christ in Lincoln. Political associate Abram J. Dittenhoefer remembered that Lincoln was quick to pick up on Douglas's differing with the import of the scriptures. It may have been that he was bothered by Douglas's use of a Q quote to denigrate Lincoln's position. Douglas said on whether a state or territory should have slavery or not, "it does not become Mr. Lincoln, or anybody else, to tell the people of Kentucky that they have no consciences, that they are living in a state of iniquity, and that they are cherishing an institution to their bosoms in violation of the law of God. Better for him to adopt the doctrine of 'judge not lest ye be judged.'" To Lincoln this use of the verse "Judge not, that ye be not judged" (Matthew 7:1/Luke 6:38) was obscene because it implied that a slave was not a person and owning slavery was simply a matter between the master and his God. Lincoln would later mock the Douglas argument by stating, "Douglas' popular sovereignty, as a matter of principle, simply is 'If one man would enslave another, neither that other, nor any third man, has a right to object.'"[51]

Lincoln would use the "judge not" quote at least three times as President. This quote appealed to his sense of predestination and notion of limited human choice. In a reply to a delegation of clergymen he said about slaveholders, "But let me forbear, remembering it is also written 'Judge not, lest ye be judged.'" He used the line again in his greatest speech, the Second Inaugural, in reference to slaveholders who he believed had started the rebellion, "but let us judge not that we be not judged." Near the end of his life, Charles Sumner, a Massachusetts Senator and friend of Mary Todd

Lincoln, recalls Lincoln using it while visiting the army near Richmond after the city had fallen to Grant and Meade. One member of his party had said that Confederate President Jefferson Davis ought to be punished. Lincoln said that, "he must repeat the words quoted in his late address, 'Judge not that ye be not judged.'"[52]

After Lincoln had lost the Senate race to Douglas, he continued to follow Douglas and speak against his popular sovereignty doctrine. In the fall of 1859, Lincoln was in Cincinnati campaigning for Republicans. He closed a rollicking speech with an appeal for Republican unity with a Q reference, "The good old maxims of the Bible are applicable, and truly applicable to human affairs, and in this as in other things, we may say here that he who is not for us is against us; he who gathereth not with us scattereth." Lincoln took this from Jesus' saying, "He that is not with me is against me; and he that gathereth not with me scattereth abroad" (Matthew 12:30/Luke 11:23).[53]

Shortly before his election as President, Lincoln found a creative use for a passage on forgiveness. According to a well-known passage in Q, "Then came Peter to him, and said, Lord, how oft shall my brother sin against me, and I forgive him? till seven times? Jesus saith unto him, I say not unto thee, Until seven times: but, Until seventy times seven" (Matthew 18:21-22/Luke 17:4). Lincoln used the passage in explaining why he would not repeat himself about intending aggression against the South. He told a Kentucky newspaper editor, "For the good men of the South—-and I regard the majority of them as such—-I have no objection to repeat seventy and seven times. But I have bad men also to deal with, both North and South—-men who are eager for something new upon which to base new misrepresentations—-men who would like to frighten me, or, at least, to fix upon me the character of timidity and cowardice."[54]

As President, Lincoln found passages from Q useful in dealing with his cabinet. Salmon Chase, Lincoln's Secretary of the Treasury, harbored presidential ambitions. Mary and many others thought he was disloyal to Lincoln because of this. Mary remembered Lincoln telling her in reference to Chase, "Do good to those who hate you and turn their ill-will into friendship."[55] Jesus says, "But I say unto you, Love your enemies, bless them that curse you, do good to them that hate you, and pray for them who despitefully use you, and persecute you" (Matthew 5:44/Luke 6:27-28).

A student of Lincoln's religion relates another episode about a Treasury Department official in which Lincoln could quickly turn to the Bible and a Q reference: "When Hugh McCulloch . . . introduced a delegation of New York bankers deferentially, he spoke of their patriotism and quoted, in conclusion, what he thought was a suitable text: 'Where the treasure is, there will the heart be also.' Reacting quickly to this fatuous use of Scripture, Lincoln without hesitation replied, 'There is another text, Mr. McCulloch, which might apply, "Where the carcass is, there will the eagles be gathered together."'" In this case Lincoln countered McCulloch's use of Q (Matthew 6:21/Luke 12:34) with his own (Matthew 24:28/Luke 17:37).[56]

In 1864, Lincoln quoted the Q material about Satan tempting Jesus. Again speaking of the pro-slavery clergymen, Lincoln stated, "to my thinking, they contemned and insulted God and His church, far more than did Satan when he tempted the Saviour with the Kingdoms of the earth. The devils attempt was no more false, and far less hypocritical."[57] Satan's tempting of Jesus at the beginning of his ministry is one of the few narrative pieces in Q, used to show Jesus' status was important enough to have Satan himself tempt him. Q reads, "Again, the devil taketh him up into an exceedingly high mountain, and showeth him all the kingdoms of the world, and the glory of them, And saith unto him, All these things will I give thee, if thou wilt fall down and worship me. Then saith Jesus unto him, Begone, Satan; for it is written, Thou shalt worship the Lord, thy God, and him only shalt thou serve" (Matthew 4:8-10/Luke 4:5-8).

Lincoln's final use of Q is memorable. In his Second Inaugural Address, Lincoln saw the war as punishment for the country's sins and as part of God's plan. As already noted, Lincoln considered divine punishment as part of the gospel. He quoted Q by saying, "Woe unto the world because of offences! For it must needs be that offences come; but woe to that man by whom the offence cometh!" Lincoln's use of this phrase (Matthew 18:7/Luke 17:1) has confused many, but it is consistent with his beliefs.[58]

Lincoln's use of Q highlights the workings of his mind. Lincoln read the gospels and discerned in the early level of the Jesus tradition the portions that were most relevant to his speeches and writings. That Lincoln did not quote the Gospel of John with its later layers of church tradition and "I am" statements shows his preference for the straightforward teachings of Jesus in the synoptic gospels. The Gospel of John was, however, very popular at the time, and the two most popular hymns in America at the time Lincoln was first running for office in the 1830s were "Rock of Ages" and "My Faith Look up to Thee," both with Gospel of John themes. Perhaps its focus on the individual's relationship with Christ rather than the larger community appealed to American individualism on the frontier.

Had Lincoln chosen to quote John he would have found an audience that was speaking his language. Lincoln, however, preferred the direct wisdom of the carpenter from Nazareth as expressed in Q and found it more applicable to his world.[59]

Chapter 5

WAR AND DEATH

Now at the end of three years struggle the nation's condition is not what
either party, or any man devised, or expected. God alone can claim it.
Abraham Lincoln, "Meditation on the Divine Will," September 2, 1862

THINGS WERE NOT GOING WELL for Lincoln and the Northern
war effort in the late summer of 1862. The Civil War had lasted more than a year, and casualty lists were lengthening. What
made matters worse was that in the early summer things had
looked so bright for the Union. After the bloody battle of Shiloh,
the western armies captured Corinth and seemed unstoppable.
New Orleans, the largest city in the South, had fallen to a joint
naval and army expedition. Much of the North Carolina coast had
fallen to the Federal Army. The Army of the Potomac under its
popular commander George B. McClellan was a few miles outside
of Richmond ready to capture the capital of the Confederacy and
administer a blow that would probably prove fatal to the nascent
nation.

A sudden reversal changed all that. The Confederate army had
stolen a march on the Federals in the west and invaded Kentucky.
Even worse, the rechristened Army of Northern Virginia, under its

new commander Robert E. Lee, had struck the Army of the Potomac hard blows in just a week, thereafter called the Seven Days Battles. Though Lee's army was severely damaged, he managed to push the Union army back twenty-five miles and save his capital. Then, in a brilliant strategic move, he launched his army directly northward and crushed a newly formed Union army at the Second Battle of Bull Run in what may have been his most spectacular performance. Lee was now free to cross the Potomac to invade Maryland and Pennsylvania.[1]

This turn of events troubled Lincoln. After a cabinet meeting on September 2, three days after Second Bull Run, Secretary of the Navy Gideon Welles wrote in his diary, "Much was said. There was more of a disturbed and desponding feeling than I have ever witnessed in council; the President was greatly distressed." Sometime during that same day, Lincoln managed to be alone. According to what he told his cabinet, he prayed to his God and made a promise. If Lee and his army were turned back from their invasion of the North, he would see it as a sign to issue his Proclamation to free the slaves and conduct the war on a much higher moral plane.[2]

The above story highlights a crucial part of Lincoln's experience as President. Though he was slowly brought into a Christian faith starting in 1849-1850, his last four years saw a blossoming of religious faith and a deepening spirituality in his life and writings. The Civil War tested Lincoln like nothing had done before. Throughout this trial he turned increasingly to his Christian worldview. By examining what Lincoln said and did in the White House, and the testimony of those who knew him, it is possible to trace this growth in Lincoln's Christian faith.

His religious faith seemed to grow as soon as he left Springfield. As Lincoln's train made its way to Washington for his inauguration, Lincoln was called on to make speech after speech. He was hamstrung in large part because he wanted to say nothing that would upset the South and further inflame the dire situation in the country. The nation was on the verge of a Civil War. Seven states in the Deep South had already seceded. More slave states were on the verge of leaving the Union as well. Lincoln was also forced to call on many local politicians and reassure the people of the North. In his speech to the New Jersey state legislature, Lincoln called on God and prayed that God would direct him to do the right things. He said, "I am exceedingly anxious that this Union, the Constitution, and the liberties of the people shall be perpetuated in accordance with the original idea for which that struggle was made, and I shall be most happy indeed if I shall be an humble instrument in the hands of the Almighty, and of this, his almost chosen people, for perpetuating the object of that great struggle."[3]

Lincoln historian Ronald White has seen Lincoln's feelings of inadequacy in relation to God in these utterances. On calling himself a "humble instrument" or an "accidental instrument," White states, "He believed that his role as a leader came not only from the people but from *the Almighty*. Lincoln contrasted *humble instrument*, as the portrayal of himself, with God, whom he described as *Almighty*."[4]

Lincoln's efforts to calm the South came to naught. In his Inaugural Address of March 4, 1861, Lincoln tried to reassure the South by appealing to the common religion both sections enjoyed. He said, "If it were admitted that you who are dissatisfied hold the right side in the dispute, there still is no single good reason for precipitate action. Intelligence, patriotism, Christianity, and a firm reliance on Him who has never yet forsaken this favored land are still competent to adjust, in the best way, all our present difficulty." Unfortunately, this was not to be.[5]

Lincoln had attended Presbyterian services in Springfield, and continued to do so when he came to Washington. However as

President he had to be careful, because attending the wrong church could send the wrong message. Lincoln told colleagues, "I wish to find a church, whose clergyman holds himself aloof from politics." On the second Sunday in March 1861, Lincoln attended the New York Avenue Presbyterian Church. Lincoln paid the rent on pew B-14, the same pew President Buchanan had used. Subsequently, Presidents McKinley, Taft, and Eisenhower have used it.[6]

The Confederate attack on Fort Sumter in April 1861 led Lincoln to call for volunteers to put down the rebellion and preserve the Union. This in turn led four more southern states to secede, and the war began. One of the stranger occurrences of the war had to be the danger Washington was in at the start of the war. As a result of a deal made during George Washington's administration, the Federal capital was surrounded by slave states, Virginia, which had just joined the Confederacy, and Maryland, which was on the brink of seceding. Due to riots in Baltimore, for a time troops and supplies could not reach Washington.

Lincoln had to be clearly worried for the safety of his capital. One of his secretaries wrote in his diary how Lincoln was so frustrated at the slow pace of reinforcements to the city that he petulantly told a few volunteers, "I don't believe there is any North. The Seventh Regiment is a myth. R. [Rhode] Island is not known in our geography any longer. *You* are the only Northern realities." These circumstances forced Lincoln to be energetic in his efforts to secure the capital and put the Northern war effort on a strong footing.[7]

While Lincoln never abandoned his belief in predestination, his need for action may have tempered it. William Lee Miller, who has studied Lincoln's character intensively, makes this comment, "We know that young Lincoln himself, when he grew up and read some books and carried on arguments, would hold for a time to a kind of fatalism, a 'doctrine of necessity,' that denied this ultimate human freedom . . . since he was not gifted with omniscience, that he was on this point wrong. We might say that his own life, which would be shot through with choices that made a difference, would disprove his own youthful theory." Miller is not exactly accurate when he characterizes Lincoln's views as a "youthful theory," as he held them his entire life. However, the events leading him to make choices tempered his philosophy for a time.[8]

He came closest to making this explicit while fretting over the safety of Washington. The aged General Winfield Scott was in charge of the army. Though he had done great service in the War of 1812 and the Mexican War, Scott was clearly past the point in which he could bear heavy responsibility. The capital was threatened by the Confederates early in the war due to the lack of preparation in the North. According to one source, Scott claimed, "It has been ordained, Mr. President, that the city shall not be captured by the Confederates." Lincoln responded with a story about a trapper who was told that "you are to die at a certain time. If you met a thousand Indians, and your death had not been ordained for that day, you would certainly escape." According to Lincoln the trapper wasn't so sure and replied that even if it was "ordained," he wanted his gun anyway. The same applied to the capital, as Lincoln said, "even if it has been ordained that the city of Washington will never be taken by the Southerners, what would we do, in case they made an attack upon the place, without men and heavy guns?"[9]

Lincoln never actually gave up his belief that events were foreordained by God, but as Miller makes clear, Lincoln did have to make choices whether he realized it or not. At the least, the above story highlights that his belief in an over-riding Providence never made him passive or lethargic.

Death came early in the war to those who Lincoln loved. Elmer Ellsworth had studied law in Lincoln's Springfield office and worked on Lincoln's presidential campaign in 1860. According to Lincoln scholar Michael Burlingame, "For years Ellsworth had been seeking an 'aged . . . gentleman . . . who only awaits a convenient opportunity to pat me on the head and adopt me as his own.'" The talented Ellsworth greatly admired Lincoln, who supposedly had "almost fatherly affection" for Ellsworth and treated him like a surrogate son. According to John Hay, Lincoln's secretary, Lincoln "loved him like a younger brother."[10]

At the beginning of the war, Ellsworth organized and became a colonel of a regiment composed of New York firemen. He drilled the regiment incessantly and modeled them on the French Zouaves. In late May 1861 Ellsworth's regiment crossed the Potomac to occupy Alexandria, Virginia, to make Washington more secure. As they marched through the streets Ellsworth spotted a Confederate flag flying from the top of a hotel. He entered the hotel and climbed to the top of the stairs to pull down the flag. As he descended the stairs, the proprietor fired a shotgun blast to his heart. The proprietor was quickly shot dead and run through with a bayonet by one of the regiment's privates, but Ellsworth lay dead. He was just twenty-four.[11]

The effect of Ellsworth's death on Lincoln was profound. Burlingame recounts Lincoln's devastation: "When a congressman expressed satisfaction that the Stars and Stripes now flew in Alexandria, Lincoln replied, '"Yes, but it was at a terrible cost!' . . . At the funeral . . . the president cried out as he viewed the corpse, 'My boy! my boy! was it necessary this sacrifice should be made!'" Lincoln turned to the consolation of religion when writing to Ellsworth's parents. He told them, "In the hope that it may be no intrusion upon the sacredness of your sorrow, I have ventured to address you this tribute to the memory of my young friend, and your brave and early fallen child. May God give you that consolation which is beyond all earthly power. Sincerely your friend in a common affliction — ." As in Eddie's death, Lincoln's faith helped sustain him. His belief that God could offer consolation would be needed in the coming year, after more losses of loved ones followed closely upon each other.[12]

Edward Baker, one of the three Whigs to serve as Congressmen in the Seventh District of Illinois, was the next to go. John Hardin, Lincoln, and Baker each represented the only Whig district in Illinois at one time or another, and all three were destined to die violent deaths. Hardin was killed during the Mexican War at the Battle of Buena Vista. Although Lincoln and Hardin were associates, they were never personally close. That was not the case with Lincoln and Baker.[13]

Baker was an English immigrant who was noted for his effective oratory. At one point, Lincoln even had to physically protect Baker when Democrats felt insulted at one of his speeches. When they threatened to take Baker off the stand, Lincoln made it clear they would have to go through him first. Lincoln's impressive size and strength were enough to intimidate any contemplating attacking Baker. Baker and Lincoln were kindred spirits in their ambition, which never got in the way of their friendship. Lincoln named his second son Eddie after Baker. By the time the Civil War began, Baker had moved to the West Coast and was Senator for Oregon, but he was a Mexican War veteran and quickly volunteered his services for the Union.[14]

In October 1861, Baker's brigade was ordered to make a demonstration against the Confederates across the Potomac at Ball's Bluff (near Leesburg). The battle was a disaster. Baker's brigade crossed the river but was quickly surrounded by Confederate forces. Many were killed or drowned when they attempted to flee. Baker himself was killed, taking a bullet while

Alexander Gardner's portrait of Lincoln and Union officers at the Antietam battle-field in October 1862. (*Library of Congress*)

trying to rally his men. One of Lincoln's associates, Charles Coffin, recalls the effect Baker's death had on Lincoln. As Lincoln went to the telegraph office to hear of news of the battle, Coffin remembers, "He almost fell as he stepped into the street, and we sprang involuntarily from our seats to render assistance, but he did not fall. With both hands pressed upon his heart he walked down the street, not returning the salute of the sentinel pacing his beat before the door."[15]

Another member of the Lincoln family made his grief known over Baker's death. Eleven-year-old Willie penned a heartfelt poem which appeared in the Washington *National Republican*. Willie was fated to join Baker in death a few months later.[16]

Willie had been born late in 1850, less then a year after Eddie's death. Named after Lincoln's brother-in-law, he appears to have been the Lincoln's favorite child. According to one scholar, Willie was "born a near-clone of his father." Intelligent, thoughtful, and kind, he even physically resembled Lincoln. A neighbor in

Springfield remembers that Willie inclined his head slightly to the left shoulder, the same way his father did. Some of Willie's letters survive. As an eight-year-old, he wrote a note to a neighbor about his trip to Chicago with his father, "This town is a very beautiful place. Me and father went to two theatres the other night. Me and father have a nice little room to ourselves. We have two little pitcher[s] on a washstand. The smallest one for me the largest one for father. We have two little towels on a top of both pitchers. The smallest one for me, the largest one for father. We have two little beds in the room. The smallest one for me, the largest one for father."[17]

Lincoln was lax when it came to disciplining his children. He did almost nothing to restrain Willie and his brother Tad, born three years later. Perhaps Eddie's death made him reluctant to deny his children anything. Herndon recalled how Lincoln would bring them to the law office. He wrote, "These children would take down the books, empty ash buckets, coal ashes, inkstand, papers, gold pens, letters, etc., in a pile and then dance on the pile. Lincoln would say nothing, so abstracted was he and so blinded to his children's faults. Had they s—t in Lincoln's hat and rubbed it on his boots, he would have laughed and thought it smart." Herndon put it simply and aptly when he said Lincoln "worshiped his children and *what* they worshiped; he loved what they loved and hated what they hated—rather, disliked what they hated, which was everything that did not bend to their freaks, whims, follies, and the like."[18]

Willie and his father were so close that Lincoln felt he could read the child's mind. When the youngest child, Tad, was upset once at being laughed at by older men for handing out religious tracts, Willie sat down and thought about how to comfort his brother. Michael Burlingame recounts what happened next: "This lasted ten or fifteen minutes, then he clasped both hands together, shut his teeth firmly over the under lip, and looked up smilingly into his father's face, who exclaimed, 'There! You have it now, my boy, have you not?' Turning to his wife's cousin, Lincoln said, 'I know every step of the process by which the boy arrived at his satisfactory solution of the question before him, as it is just such slow methods I attain results.'"[19]

In early February 1862, Willie was sick. Washington's climate was never healthy, and Willie was taken ill with an infection, probably typhoid or malaria, likely from drinking the unclean water in the city. Both parents nursed the boy as best as they could, which must have reminded them of their ordeal with Eddie. Willie seemed to improve, but the late afternoon of the twentieth, he slipped away.[20]

Both parents were devastated. John Nicolay, one of Lincoln's secretaries, wrote in his journal, "At about 5 o'clock this afternoon, I was lying half asleep on the sofa in my office, when his entrance aroused me. 'Well, Nicolay,' said he choking with emotion, 'my boy is gone—he is actually gone!' and bursting into tears, turned and went into his own office." Willie's death would haunt both Lincolns for the rest of their lives. The memory of his lost son even came to Lincoln in his dreams. He once asked an associate, "Did you ever dream of some lost friend and feel that you were having a sweet communion with him, and yet have a consciousness that it was not a reality? . . . That is the way I dream of my lost boy Willie." On the last day of his life, Lincoln would say to his wife, "We must *both*, be more cheerful in the future—between the war and the loss of our darling Willie—we have both, been very miserable."[21]

Former slave Lizzie Keckley, who worked for the Lincolns as a seamstress and was a confidante of Mary, remembered the effect Willie's death had on Lincoln. She also was witness to Lincoln's thoughts regarding Willie's fate. A few years later she wrote of the scene immediately following Willie's death, "God called the beautiful spirit home, and the house of joy was turned into the house of mourning. . . . I never saw a man so bowed down with grief. He came to the bed, lifted the cover from the face of his child, gazed at it long and earnestly, murmuring, 'My poor boy, he was too good for this earth. God has called him home. I know that he is much better off in heaven, but then we loved him so. It is hard, hard to have him die!'" Just as the belief that Eddie may be in heaven had earlier comforted Lincoln, here he asserts that God "called" Willie "home" and that he is "much better off in heaven."[22]

Lincoln found that hope of Willie being in a better place also in Shakespeare. Lincoln had been a reader and admirer of Shakespeare since his youth. On a trip to Fort Monroe after Willie's death, Lincoln turned to Constance's lament for her son in *King John*:

> And, father cardinal, I have heard you say
> That we shall see and know our friends in heaven:
> If that be true, I shall see my boy again.[23]

Just as Eddie's death had deepened Lincoln's religious faith, Willie's led to further ruminations for Lincoln on the nature of God. A journalist later remembered Lincoln's growing faith as President. Noah Brooks said, "Once or twice, speaking to me of the change which had come upon him, he said, while he could not fix any definite time, yet it was after he came here, and I am very positive that in his own mind he identified it with about the time of Willie's death." Mary told Herndon after the war, "he was a religious man always, as I think: he first thought—to say think—about this subject was when Willie died—never before." She is clearly in error, since the man who had read *The Christian's Defence* and discussed its contents with its author could hardly be said to have been uninterested in religion. David Donald has perceptively observed, "That statement perhaps told more about the

lack of intimacy in the Lincoln marriage than it did about the President's
state of mind." In any case, Mary was
probably conflating the effects of the
deaths of both boys on Lincoln
because she later told Rev. James
Smith that Lincoln was directed
toward religion at Eddie's death.
Either way, the loss of a beloved
child turned Lincoln's thoughts to
the hereafter and the hope that his
sons had been granted eternal life.[24]

William "Willie" Wallace Lincoln,
Abraham Lincoln's third son.
(*Library of Congress*)

Willie's funeral was held in the
East Room of the White House.
Mary Lincoln could not bring her-
self to attend. The commander-in-
chief of the Union Army, General McClellan, was in tears. As the
casket was taken to the hearse, it was followed by a group of children who attended the same Sunday school as Willie. Reverend
Phineas D. Gurley, pastor of the New York Avenue Presbyterian
Church, preached the sermon. Gurley told the audience, "The
beloved youth, whose death we now and here lament, was a child
of bright intelligence and of peculiar promise. He possessed many
excellent qualities of mind and heart, which greatly endeared him,
not only to his family circle . . . but to his youthful companions,
and to all his acquaintances and friends." Gurley also used a
melancholy reference to the Old Testament, "It is easy to see how
a child, thus endowed, would in the course of eleven years,
entwine himself around the hearts of those who knew him best;
nor can we wonder that the grief of his affectionate mother to-day
is like that of Rachel weeping for her children, and refusing to be
comforted because they were not."[25]

Later in the sermon Gurley used some of the same Gospel material concerning bereavement that Lincoln had used in the past. Gurley quoted the passage, "Of such is the kingdom of heaven," that had so comforted Lincoln at the death of Eddie and was engraved on Eddie's tombstone. Gurley said, "That departure was a sore bereavement to the parents and brothers; but while they weep, they also rejoice in the confidence that their loss is the unspeakable and eternal gain of the departed; for they believe, as well they may, that he has gone to Him who said: 'Suffer the little children to come unto me, and forbid them not, for of such is the kingdom of heaven.'" Gurley then used the same quote that Lincoln had written to John Johnston as their father lay dying eleven years before: "Nor a sparrow falls to the ground without His direction; much less any one of the human family, for we are of more value than many sparrows."26

Gurley continued with the standard explanation to parents for the loss of children. He said, "A mysterious dealing they may consider it, but still it is His dealing; and while they mourn He is saying to them, as the Lord Jesus once said to his Disciples when they were perplexed by his conduct, 'What I do ye know not now, but ye shall know hereafter.'" Lincoln was moved enough by what Gurley said to request a copy of his address to read over and give to his friends. The Lincolns also gave Gurley an ebony cane with a gold head inscribed with roses, bearing an inscription from the President and his wife.27

As President, Lincoln still craved the intellectual debates on religious topics that he had had with Smith in Springfield. He found a willing partner in Gurley. The President even invited him over to the White House early in the morning to continue to talk about theology after a long discussion the previous night. According to Gurley, as he left the White House that morning one of his parishioners asked what he was doing there so early in the morning. Gurley remembered in an unpublished manuscript, "'Why doctor,' said my friend, 'it is not nine o'clock. What are you doing at the Executive Mansion?' To this I replied, 'Mr. Lincoln and I have been having a morning chat.' 'On the war, I suppose?' 'Far from it,' said I. 'We have been talking of the state of the soul after death. That is a subject of which Mr. Lincoln never tires. I have had a great many conversations with him on the subject.'" Gurley added, "'This morning, however, I was a listener, as Mr. Lincoln did all the talking.'" Lincoln sometimes attended Gurley's prayer meetings, held in the church basement on Thursdays. When too many people were interrupting the meetings to see Lincoln and ask for political favors, Gurley suggested that Lincoln stay in the pastor's study and listen to what was being said. Gurley reported that Lincoln told him that "he had received great comfort from the meetings."[28]

Years later, Gurley would remember Lincoln's faith in a conversation with another minister. William Barton has rightfully concluded that Gurley's account was basically accurate. Barton writes, "Dr. Gurley's testimonies to the religious development of Lincoln's life were conservative, and bear upon their face marks of trustworthiness. There are no extravagant claims; no florid and declamatory theological affirmations." When asked about Lincoln's religious thought, Gurley considered him "sound not only on the truth of the Christian religion but on all its fundamental doctrines and teaching. . . . After the death of his son Willie, and his visit to the battlefield of Gettysburg, he said . . . that he had lost confidence in everything but God, and that he now believed his heart was changed, and that he loved the Savior, and if he was not deceived in himself, it was his intention soon to make a profession of religion." The last part about Lincoln making a "profession of religion" is probably a gloss on Lincoln's words by either Gurley or Rev. James Reed, who recorded this testimony. The sentiments were probably Lincoln's, though recounted dramatically by Reed to make a point.[29]

Another clergyman that Lincoln was close to as President was Methodist Bishop Matthew Simpson. Simpson had dealings with Lincoln in regards to the lack of Methodist appointments to Federal offices in relation to their relatively large numbers in the general population. Lincoln respected Simpson, appreciating his fierce patriotism and support of the President's policies on emancipation. Lincoln even asked Simpson to stand in for him at the opening of the Philadelphia Sanitary Fair in 1864. Later, Simpson gave a moving eulogy of Lincoln at his burial in Springfield.

Because Simpson made no pretense of knowing Lincoln's exact religious views, what he does say about the subject is reasonable and believable. "This I know, however, he read the Bible frequently, loved it for its great truths, and profound teachings; and he tried to be guided by its precepts. He believed in Christ, the Savior of sinners, and I think he was sincerely trying to bring his life into the principles of revealed religion. Certainly, if there ever was a man who illustrated some of the principles of pure religion, that man was our departed President." Simpson then spoke of how, on the last day of his life, Lincoln had been prepared to let many of the Confederate leadership escape after the war. Simpson compared Lincoln to Christ on the cross in his forgiveness. Using the somewhat disputed text of Luke 23:34, he said, "So that in his expiring acts he was saying, 'Father, forgive them; they know not what they do.'"[30]

Not long after the death of Willie in February 1862, Lincoln had floated a compensated emancipation plan for the slave states that had stayed loyal to the union. His idea was to pay the states to free their slaves gradually. Such a move, he felt, would help the war effort by denying the South hope that they could get support from the border states. It would also fulfill his "oft-expressed *personal* wish that all men every where could be free."[31]

Many Christian groups were pressuring Lincoln to proceed with emancipation. There was no need to persuade him of the injustice of slavery. As he told one correspondent, "I am naturally anti-slavery. If slavery is not wrong, nothing is wrong. I can not remember when I did not so think or feel." When a Chicago delegation presented Lincoln with a memorial that stated emancipation was God's will, he somewhat tongue-in-cheek replied:

> The subject presented in the memorial is one upon which I have thought much for weeks past, and I may even say for months. I am approached with the most opposite opinions and advice, and that by religious men, who are equally certain that they represent the Divine will. I am sure that either the one or the other class is mistaken in that belief, and perhaps in some respects both. I hope it will not be irreverent for me to say that if it is probable that God would reveal his will to others, on a point so connected with my duty, it might be supposed he would reveal it directly to me; for, unless I am more deceived in myself than I often am, it is my earnest desire to know the will of Providence in this matter. And if I can learn what it is I will do it! These are not, however, the days of miracles, and I suppose it will be granted that I am not to expect a direct revelation. I must study the plain physical facts of the case, ascertain what is possible and learn what appears to be wise and right.

Lincoln continued, "I admit that slavery is the root of the rebellion, or at least its *sine qua non*. The ambition of politicians may have instigated them to act, but they would have been impotent without slavery as their instrument." What the delegation didn't know was that Lincoln had a proclamation of emancipation in his desk, ready to be issued. He was simply waiting for the right time.[32]

Lincoln could issue a decree of emancipation only as commander-in-chief during wartime. He was careful to justify it legally because he was concerned that Chief Justice Roger B. Taney, architect of the Dred Scott infamy, would declare it unconstitutional. He first broached the subject in July 1862, but was told by Secretary of State William Seward to wait until a more propitious time. Seward reasoned that if Lincoln issued a proclamation freeing the slaves shortly after the defeat of the Seven Days Battles, it would seem to be an act of desperation. Perhaps Seward knew that Lincoln would appreciate a biblical reference, because, as Allen Guelzo writes, "This decree would, Seward said, playing on a biblical simile, look like 'the government stretching forth its hands to Ethiopia, instead of Ethiopia stretching forth her hands to the government' or like a 'last *shriek* on the retreat.'"[33]

After Lee crushed the Federal Army under John Pope at Second Bull Run in late August, he invaded Maryland. Hoping to detach the slave state Maryland from the Union, he then intended to push forward and invade Pennsylvania. This strategy came to naught when McClellan pursued Lee and gave him battle along Antietam Creek on September 17, 1862, still the bloodiest single day in American history. Lee's army, still intact, was so battered he was forced to retreat across the Potomac to Virginia. Lincoln felt this was enough of a victory to issue his Proclamation.[34]

Using Antietam as an occasion was only part of Lincoln's careful timing. It is one of the most amazing examples of Lincoln's religiosity while President. The Secretary of the Treasury, Salmon P. Chase, joined the entire cabinet and the President on September 22. Chase recorded in his diary how Lincoln had started the meeting with some humor before going into the serious matter of emancipation. (Chase's diary is probably trustworthy since he wrote down these events on the day they occurred.) "All the members of the Cabinet were in attendance. There was some general talk; and the President mentioned that Artemus Ward had sent him his book. Proposed to read a chapter which he thought very funny. Read it, and seemed to enjoy it very much—The Heads also (except Stanton) of course. The Chapter was 'Highhanded Outrage at Utica.'" The humorous story Lincoln read is a satirical piece poking fun at the absurdly pious. It is about a man who was so overcome with rage at seeing Judas in a wax sculpture of the Last Supper that he ran up and pulled Judas down and started to pound him. He told the sculptor, "I tell you, old man, that Judas Iscarrot can't show hisself in Utiky by a darn site!" Lincoln may have picked that story to show that he was no religious fanatic with the shocking thing he was going to say next.[35]

Chase then continued with the cabinet meeting as Lincoln put down the Artemus Ward book and commenced the business at hand. He writes:

> The President then took a graver tone and said: -
> "Gentlemen: I have, as you are aware, thought a great deal about the relation of this war to Slavery; and you all remember that, several weeks ago, I read to you an Order I had prepared on this subject, which, on account of objections made by some of you, was not issued. Ever since then, my mind has been much occupied with this subject, and I have thought all along that the time for acting on it might very probably come. I think the time has come now. I wish it were a better time. I wish that we were in a better condition. The action of the army against the rebels has not been quite what I should have best liked. But they have been driv-

en out of Maryland, and Pennsylvania is no longer in danger of invasion. When the rebel army was at Frederick, I determined, as soon as it should be driven out of Maryland, to issue a Proclamation of Emancipation such as I thought most likely to be useful. I said nothing to any one; but I made the promise to myself, and (hesitating a little)—to my Maker. The rebel army is now driven out, and I am going to fulfill that promise."

Lincoln was waiting for a sign from God of when to act. The incident was further confirmed by Francis Carpenter, who was at the White House to paint a picture of this cabinet meeting. Chase characteristically gave himself a more prominent role in the meeting. Carpenter related what Chase had told him, "the President entered upon the business before them, by saying that 'the time for the annunciation of the emancipation policy could be no longer delayed. Public sentiment,' he thought, 'would sustain it—many of his warmest friends and supporters demanded it—*and he had promised his God that he should do it.'* When Chase asked if he understood this correctly, Mr. Lincoln replied, '*I made a solemn vow before God, that if General Lee was driven back from Pennsylvania, I would crown the results by the declaration of freedom to the slaves.*'"[36]

Chase was not the only one to hear Lincoln's remark. Gideon Welles also recorded the incident in his diary:

> The subject was the Proclamation for emancipating slaves after a certain date, in States that shall then be in rebellion. For several weeks the subject has been suspended, but the President says never lost sight of. When it was submitted, and now in taking up the Proclamation, the President stated that the question

was finally decided, the act and the consequences were his, but that he felt it due to us to make us acquainted with the fact and to invite criticism on the paper he had prepared. There were, he had found, not unexpectedly, some differences in the Cabinet, but he had, after ascertaining in his own way the views of each and all, individually and collectively, formed his own conclusions and made his own decision. In the course of the discussion on this paper, which was long, earnest, and, on the general principle involved, harmonious, he remarked that he had made a vow, a covenant, that if God gave us the victory in the approaching battle, he would consider it an indication of Divine will, and that it was his duty to move forward in the cause of emancipation. It might be thought strange, he said, that he had in this way submitted the disposal of matters when the way was not clear to his mind what he should do. God had decided this question in favor of the slaves. He was satisfied it was right, was confirmed and strengthened in his action by the vow and the results.

Welles later said of the day's events, "he had in this way submitted the disposal of the subject to a Higher Power, and abided by what seemed the Supreme Will." It is clear that Lincoln's uncharacteristic pledge made quite an impression on his hearers.[37]

Was Lincoln acting, as one scholar put it, like the Roman Emperor Constantine or the Puritan warrior Oliver Cromwell? Did Lincoln feel he had a special calling to interpret the Almighty's intentions for what he should do as President? A crucial difference exists between Lincoln's actions and Constantine's or Cromwell's. The President made a personal vow to God to issue the proclamation. Lincoln took the active role, in promising God to do something and hoping that God would sustain his wishes by a sign. Lincoln did not claim God initiated the idea to issue a proclamation freeing the slaves. Lincoln seems to have been embarrassed by the presumptuousness of what he said, and he quickly doubted he could read God's intentions. At an event celebrating the emancipation two days later, Lincoln said, "I can only trust in God I have made no mistake."[38]

Lincoln's general belief was that it was almost sacrilegious to claim God supported him or his positions. Lincoln told Maine's Governor Lot Morrill, "I don't know but that God has created some one man great enough to comprehend the whole of this stupendous crisis and transaction from beginning to end, and endowed him with sufficient wisdom to manage and direct it. I confess I do not fully understand and foresee it all. But I am placed here where I am obliged to the best of my poor ability to deal with it." He even told his friend Orville Browning, "Suppose God is against us in our view on the subject of slavery in this country, and our method of dealing with it?" He could never shake the disdain he had for people such as Robert Burns's "Holy Willie" who were so sure that they knew they were the "elect."[39]

Bishop Simpson told a telling anecdote about Lincoln's views on the matter in his eulogy: "'To a minister who said he hoped the Lord was on our side, he replied that it gave him no concern whether the Lord was on our side or not, 'For,' he added, 'I know the Lord is always on the side of the right;' and with deep feeling added, 'But God is my witness that it is my constant anxiety and prayer that both myself and this nation should be on the Lord's side.'" Lincoln would admit that ultimately only God knew the divine plan for this world. He told another minister during the war, "God only knows the issue of this business. He has destroyed nations from the map of history for their sins. Nevertheless, my hopes prevail generally above my fears for our Republic. The times are dark, the spirits of ruin are abroad in all their power, and the mercy of God alone can save us."[40]

In his dealings with the Quakers, Lincoln wrote two notes which shed light on his attitude about God's purposes and how he saw his own role. After an October 1862 meeting with the Society of Friends, he expressed his pleasure at the interview and spoke of "being a humble instrument in the hands of our Heavenly Father, as I am, and as we all are, to work out his great purposes, I have desired that all my works and acts may be according to his will, and that it might be so, I have sought his aid—but if after endeavoring to do my best in the light which he affords me, I find my efforts fail, I must believe that for some purpose unknown to me, he wills it otherwise." He wrote them again two years later on the same theme, "The purposes of the Almighty are perfect, and must prevail, though we erring mortals may fail to accurately perceive them in advance. . . . Meanwhile we must work earnestly in the best lights he gives us, trusting that so working still conduces to the great ends he ordains."[41]

At some point during the war Lincoln felt the need to clarify for himself the divine purpose of all this suffering. Taking a scrap of paper, he decided to write down his thoughts:

> The will of God prevails. In great contests each party claims to act in accordance with the will of God. Both may be, and one must be wrong. God can not be for, and against the same thing at the same time. In the present civil war it is quite possible that God's purpose is something different from the purpose of either party—- and yet the human instrumentalities, working just as they do, are of the best adaptation to effect His purpose. I am almost ready to say this is probably true—that God wills this contest, and wills that it shall not end yet. By

his mere quiet power, on the minds of the now contest-
ants, He could have either saved or destroyed the Union
without a human contest. Yet the contest began. And
having begun He could give the final victory to either
side any day. Yet the contest proceeds.

This note was never intended to be seen by anyone else, and was
not discovered by Lincoln's secretaries until after his death. At that
time, one of them said it was "penned in the awful sincerity of a
perfectly honest soul trying to bring itself into closer communion
with its Maker." This note was not for public consumption, but for
Lincoln himself as he wrestled with the concepts of predestination
and the mysteries of God's purpose in this world.[42]

The most explicit statement Lincoln made about God's role in
shaping his action on earth is his April 1864 letter to Albert
Hodges. Lincoln had to explain emancipation to the people of
Kentucky, a slave state that had stayed loyal to the Union. Lincoln
wrote, "I add a word which was not in the verbal conversation. In
telling this tale I attempt no compliment to my own sagacity. I
claim not to have controlled events, but confess plainly that events
have controlled me. Now at the end of three years struggle the
nation's condition is not what either party, or any man devised, or
expected. God alone can claim it." One may surmise that Lincoln
was attempting to soften the blow of emancipation by claiming it
was inevitable, God's will, and as such, reflects solely political
rather than theological implications. This supposition is mistaken.
Too many similar statements of belief by Lincoln show he was not
merely playing politics.[43]

Mentions of God are sprinkled liberally throughout Lincoln's
speeches and public proclamations as President. However, one
must be careful about drawing conclusions about Lincoln's personal religious feelings from these. As one scholar noted, "It must

be stressed that Lincoln's speeches were political speeches, not personal confessions. . . . In Lincoln's speeches one cannot find personal piety divorced from politics."[44]

The above statement needs to be qualified because Lincoln's speeches do not have key elements of purely political piety. He never told the public what it wanted to hear. His speeches never proclaimed the North's moral superiority over the South. His public pronouncements also lack the Cromwellian rhetoric of God smiting the enemies of the Union, which Lincoln would have employed had he been merely using God to make politic points. H. L. Mencken, who was something of a professional cynic, got it wrong when he once remarked that Lincoln's "most memorable feat, was his appointment of the Lord God Jehova to the honorary chairmanship of the Republican National Committee." This statement is more telling of Mencken's antagonism toward religion than it is of anything Lincoln said. Lincoln's personal reluctance to criticize anyone publicly for religious reasons goes back to his own Congressional campaign in which that tactic was used against him.[45]

One of Lincoln's first uses of religion publicly was his Proclamation of a day of fasting following the Union defeat at Bull Run in July 1861. Lincoln told the people of America, "And whereas, when our own beloved Country, once, by the blessing of God, united, prosperous and happy, is now afflicted with faction and civil war, it is peculiarly fit for us to recognize the hand of God in this terrible visitation, and in sorrowful remembrance of our own faults and crimes as a nation and as individuals, to humble ourselves before Him, and to pray for His mercy."[46]

Lincoln urged "humility" for the country. He continued to see punishment as part of God's system. When Lincoln wrote "to pray that we may be spared further punishment, though most justly deserved," he was simply stating what he had for a long time believed privately. The American people were too used to hearing of the grace and redemption of Christianity and had forgotten about the punishing aspect of a just God. Lincoln thought the shock of military defeat would be enough to wake up Americans from their spiritual complacency.

He also had no problem invoking God in a way that would make many twenty-first-century commentators blanch. The entrenchment of the separation between church and state and the general rise of secularism has made a proclamation like the one above unthinkable. One student of Lincoln, Joseph Fornieri, has called Lincoln's views "Biblical Republicanism." The sixteenth president had no problem using the Bible as a normative code of morality and ethics. His use of the Q material in the Sermon of the Mount was natural to him and to the many Americans who thought of the Bible as the ideal of what human behavior should be. Fornieri gives high marks to Lincoln for combining reason and revelation. He writes, "Because reason is the common language of public discourse in a nonsectarian society, leaders who invoke religion should explore Lincoln's example in translating the basic moral precepts of the Bible into rational terms."[47]

Giving thanks to God would also be a theme of Lincoln's proclamations. After the Union victories in Tennessee at Fort Henry and Donelson, and the failure of the Confederate counterattack at Shiloh, Lincoln offered this proclamation, "It is therefore recommended to the People of the United States that, at their next weekly assemblages in their accustomed places of public worship . . . they especially acknowledge and render thanks to our Heavenly Father for these inestimable blessings." Even if Secretary of State Seward was the author of these proclamations, Lincoln allowed them to carry his name.[48]

Lincoln's suggestion that people offer thanks at "their next weekly assemblages" where they usually "worship" shows the nonsectarian nature of Lincoln's religious proclamations. Notably he did not mention Sunday as the day of public worship; Lincoln had great respect for the Jewish tradition and had no wish to exclude Jews because they did not believe in Jesus Christ. When his Secretary of War rejected a rabbi for the position of chaplain of a regiment because the law required that chaplains be Christians, Lincoln wrote the rabbi, "My dear Sir: I find that there are several particulars in which the present law in regard to Chaplains is supposed to be deficient, all of which I now design presenting to the appropriate Committee of Congress. I shall try to have a new law broad enough to cover what is desired by you in behalf of the Israelites." His most famous example of tolerance toward Judaism was his rejection of General Grant's order expelling Jewish traders from his military lines.[49]

Lincoln was most explicit in applying Christianity to policy when he wrote Secretary of War Edwin M. Stanton about his rules for pardon: "On principle I dislike an oath which requires a man to swear he *has* not done wrong. It rejects the Christian principle of forgiveness on terms of repentance. I think it is enough if the man does no wrong *hereafter*."[50]

As to Lincoln's personal piety during this period, there are numerous witnesses to his basic Christianity. Predictably Herndon clung for the rest of his life to the letter he received from John Nicolay written shortly after Lincoln's death, "Mr. Lincoln did not to my knowledge in any way change his religious ideas, opinions, or beliefs from the time he left Springfield to the day of his death. I do not know just what they were, never heard him explain in detail; but I am very sure he gave no outward indication of his mind having undergone any change in that regard while here." Although Nicolay did not know what Lincoln's religious beliefs were before he came to Washington, while he was President they matured and deepened, but his proto-orthodox Christianity was already in place by about 1850.[51]

One of the main witnesses to Lincoln's beliefs as President is his best friend Joshua Speed. Speed told the story quoted above about Lincoln telling him to take the Bible on "reason" and "faith." Speed was witness to another important incident concerning Lincoln's religious outlook which occurred shortly before Lincoln's death and has often been misinterpreted by historians. In his first interviews with Herndon, Speed mentioned the event but fleshed it out in an 1866 letter. He spoke of two women who had been waiting to see Lincoln to ask Lincoln for the release of their sons for resisting the draft in western Pennsylvania. Lincoln was touched by the plight of their sons and felt that all the resisters from the area "had suffered enough" and decided to "turn out the *flock*." The women were so overcome with emotion that one of them grabbed Lincoln's hand and cried. She said, "Mr Lincoln— I shall never see you again till we meet in Heaven." According to Speed, Lincoln replied, "I am afraid with all my troubles I shall never get there—But if I do I will find you - That you wish me to get there is the best wish you could make for me—good bye."[52]

Lincoln's assertion that he may never get to heaven has been used as evidence that he still was a strong skeptic up till his death, but this story shows nothing of the kind. David Donald uses it to show Lincoln disbelieved in the afterlife, but omits the part where Lincoln says, "But if I do I will find you." It is actually another illustration of Lincoln's humility that was evident throughout his life, on a par with his saying that he could not know God's will directly.[53]

In the same letter quoted above Speed tells Herndon about Lincoln's undeniable early skepticism of the Christian religion but also of the change he saw in Lincoln in the White House. He stated, "I think that when I knew Mr L he was skeptical as to the great truths of the Christian religion. I think that after he was elected President, he sought to become a believer—and to make the Bible a preceptor to his faith and a guide for his conduct."[54]

Another important witness is Isaac Arnold, an old associate of Lincoln from his days as an Illinois lawyer. While Lincoln was President, Arnold was a Republican Congressman who was extremely loyal to the President. During the dark days of the summer of 1864, a fellow Republican Congressman, Pennsylvanian Thaddeus Stevens, said that Arnold was the only "Lincoln Congressman" there was. Arnold was one of the few people who knew him personally to write a biography of Lincoln. He even represented Mary Todd Lincoln in her 1875 insanity trial.

Arnold's 1884 volume, *The Life of Abraham Lincoln*, has valuable firsthand information including Lincoln's religious views. No doubt speaking of the things Herndon had said about the topic, Arnold wrote, "It is very strange that any reader of Lincoln's speeches and writings should have the hardihood to charge him with a want of religious feeling. No more reverent Christian than he ever sat in the executive chair, not excepting Washington. He was by nature religious; full of religious sentiment. The veil between him and the supernatural was very thin. It is not claimed that he was orthodox. For creeds and dogmas he cared little." When it came to the actual core beliefs, Arnold confidently said, "But in the great fundamental principles of religion, of the Christian religion, he was a firm believer. Belief in the existence of God, the immortality of the soul, in the Bible as the revelation of God to man, in the efficacy and duty of prayer, in reverence towards the Almighty, and in love and charity to man, was the basis of his religion."[55]

The painter Francis Carpenter also gave some testimony on Lincoln's religion. He was in the White House for a period of six months in 1864, but was probably not as intimate with Lincoln as he would have liked the readers of his 1866 book to believe. There he said, "My access to the official chambers was made nearly as free as that of the private secretaries." However, after his book came out Mary Todd Lincoln wrote, "This man Carpenter never had a dozen interviews with the late president and the latter complained to me more than once that C. presumed upon the privilege he had give C . . . C. intruded frequently into Mr L's office, when time was too precious to be idled."

The truth is probably somewhere in the middle. At the least Lincoln was comfortable enough to recite his favorite melancholy poetry to Carpenter. This may have led to discussions of the divine. Carpenter was forced to admit, "I would scarcely call Mr. Lincoln a *religious* man, —and yet I believe him to have been a sincere *Christian*. A constitutional tendency to dwell upon sacred things, an emotional nature which finds ready expression in religious conversation and revival meetings, the culture and development of the devotional element till the expression of such thought and experience becomes habitual, were not among his characteristics." Yet of Lincoln's religious character Carpenter could still write, "And yet, aside from emotional expression, I believe no man had a more abiding sense of dependence on God, or faith in the Divine government, and in the power and ultimate triumph of Truth and Right in the world." Later, speaking of Lincoln's "Christian character," Carpenter states, "If his daily life and various public addresses and writings do not show this, surely nothing can."[56]

The witness who claimed the most about Lincoln's Christianity as President is Noah Brooks, a war correspondent who sent long letters to the *Sacramento Union* under the pen name "Castine." He first came to Washington in December 1862 to cover the White House. Brooks had met Lincoln earlier in Illinois while covering the 1856 presidential campaign. He agreed with the President's politics and got along well with him. Brooks's wife had died shortly before he came to Washington and the Lincolns, having lost Willie earlier that year, may have felt a natural sympathy with the young widower. Mary Todd Lincoln lobbied for Brooks to become Lincoln's private secretary when John Nicolay was due to leave for Europe, but the assassination intervened.[57]

In Washington, Brooks curiously first saw Lincoln while attending church in November 1862. In his first dispatch Brooks told his readers of the effect the cares of office had taken on Lincoln as the President attended church for spiritual solace.[58]

Brooks was on hand when the President won re-election and was privy to a confession of Lincoln on the power of prayer. Brooks told his readers that Lincoln stated, "I should be the veriest shallow and self-conceited blockhead upon the footstool if, in my discharge of the duties which are put upon me in this place, I should hope to get along without the wisdom which comes from God and not from men." Lincoln again showed his knowledge of the Bible by referring to the earth as a "footstool." The Gospel of Matthew states that no person should swear by heaven because this is where God lives on earth, "for it is his footstool" (Matthew 5:35). Brooks went on to add, "In many loyal hearts these simple words of trust will find a responsive thrill. God give him grace!"[59]

The last part of that quote illustrates why many historians have had trouble accepting the testimony of Brooks. Brooks himself was a highly religious man, and may have wanted to make Lincoln a pious example to the world. Often the argument is made that Lincoln would not have discussed such a sensitive matter, but the evidence is that Lincoln did open himself up to Brooks as a confidant. For example, after Brooks read to Lincoln a telegraph recounting the Union retreat after the May 1863 battle of Chancellorsville, he remembered, "The appearance of the President, as I read aloud these fateful words, was piteous. Never as long as I knew him, did he seem to be so broken, so dispirited and so ghostlike. Clasping his hands behind his back, he walked up and down the room, saying, 'My God! my God! What will the country say! What will the country say!'" Lincoln could be so unguarded because Brooks was someone he felt he could trust.[60]

In any case, Brooks gave specifics regarding Lincoln's Christian beliefs in a letter he wrote to a minister shortly after the assassination. He remembered, "I am glad now that I never hesitated, when proper occasion offered, to talk with him upon religious matters, for I think that the best evidences of his belief in Christ are those which I derived in free and easy conversations with him. . . . He told me that the prayers of the people had greatly sustained him, and that he had always sought from God, the source of knowledge and wisdom, that strength which he needed. This he often repeated to others, substantially." Brooks gave a similar but expanded recounting a few years later in a letter. He even suggested that Lincoln was ready to join a church formally by baptism. There is no reason to believe this is true, and is more likely a hopeful surmise on the part of Brooks. In 1872, Brooks wrote that Lincoln had "a hope of blessed immortality through Jesus Christ." Brooks continued, "His language seemed not that of an inquirer, but of one who had a prior settled belief in the fundamental doctrines of the Christian religion. . . . I absorbed the firm conviction that Mr. Lincoln was at heart a Christian man, believed in the Savior, and was seriously considering the step which would formally connect him with the visible Church on earth."[61]

While Brooks did not know Lincoln from the start of his stay in Washington as President, he felt the experience of being President had led to an evolution in Lincoln's religious views, and remembered Lincoln telling him as much. According to Brooks, these heavy duties of being President led Lincoln to say, "I have been driven many times upon my knees by the overwhelming conviction that I had nowhere else to go. My own wisdom and that of all about me seemed insufficient for that day." Brooks would also write, "Afterward, referring to what he called a change of heart, he said that he did not remember any precise time when he passed through any special change of purpose or of heart; but he would say that his own election to office, and the crisis immediately following, influentially determined him in what he called a 'process of crystallization.'" The use of the word "crystallization" is illustrative because it assumes a previous foundation of religion. Brooks would have been unaware of the effects Dr. Smith had on Lincoln, but perhaps he sensed it in the conversations he had with Lincoln.[62]

William O. Stoddard was another person who saw Lincoln close up and commented on the President's Christianity. Stoddard was a journalist in Illinois who wished to be appointed Lincoln's secretary. He didn't get that position, but he was appointed a clerk in the Interior Department. His job was to sign Lincoln's name to land patents, but the war quickly curtailed this demand on his time, and he was detailed to the White House as an assistant secretary opening the voluminous mail the President received. He was also invaluable for the White House staff, not least because he was one of the few people that could get along with the President's wife. Stoddard made much of his experience with Lincoln. He lived well into old age and wrote a number of books on Lincoln. Like many, though, he wanted to give the impression he was on more intimate terms with Lincoln than he really was.[63]

Shortly after the war, Stoddard wrote in series of sketches of his career in the White House, "[Lincoln's] religion was in his faith and in his life rather than in any profession. So far as I know, his religious belief or opinions never, at any period of his life, took the shape of a formal profession. His nature was not at all enthusiastic, and his mind was subject to none of the fevers which pass with the weak and shallow for religious fervor, and in this, as in all other things, he was thoroughly honest to assume which he did not feel." Stoddard also stressed Lincoln's lack of concern about differences between Christian sects: "He was not, however, a man to pay much attention to or care much about the thin walls of separation between different denominations." Stoddard's remarks back up what many others said about Lincoln's lack of a formal creed and the premium he put on reason.[64]

Of Lincoln's specific religious beliefs Stoddard would later write, "I cannot at this moment recall any distinct assertions made by Mr. Lincoln, relating to matters of his religious belief, but we do not gather our conceptions of the religion of other men altogether from their repetitions of any formal creed and this I can say, that after being with him daily for three years and a half. . . . I am convinced this day that, in the best and truest sense, Abraham Lincoln was a Christian." He went on to discount much of what Herndon had said regarding Lincoln's lack of faith in his youth: "Mr. Lincoln, first, believed in the God he prayed to, and on whose help he confidently relied; second, believed in the authority of the book which he quoted as Divine law, and whose mandate he not only strove to honor in his own person, but in the respect required for them of those under his authority." Stoddard then went on to add, "that whatever may have been Mr. Lincoln's vagaries of opinion in former days, the rubbish of New Salem atheism was burned out of him in the fiery furnace of long trial, great sorrow, and compelled acknowledgment of Divine Power." Stoddard acknowledges Lincoln may have been skeptical as a youth but insists the Lincoln Herndon knew was not the Lincoln of the White House.[65]

Two other witnesses were refreshingly less self-assured in their analysis of Lincoln, yet both intimated that the Lincoln they knew in the White House was indeed a Christian. Lincoln would often spend time at the War Department building in the telegraph office to read the news from the front and developed a good relationship with many of the men who worked there. Lincoln would often joke and tell his stories in the relaxed atmosphere. David Homer Bates was one of those men, and years later he wrote, "if love be the fulfilling of the law of Christ, Abraham Lincoln, in his day and generation, was the nearly perfect human example of the operation of that law. I do not refer directly to his belief in a divine Being, nor in orthodox creeds, although his manifold utterances on the subject of slavery . . . must ever proclaim to the thinking world the fact that at the very root of his spiritual being he held sacred the teaching of the Bible."[66]

Orville Hickman Browning, a good friend of Lincoln and an Illinois Senator, was also circumspect about Lincoln's religion. He wrote in a letter, "I know Mr Lincoln was a firm believer in a superintending Providence, and in super-natural agencies and events. I know that he believed the destinies of men were, or at least, that his own destiny was, shaped, and controlled, by an intelligence and power higher and greater than his own, and which he could neither control or thwart." That belief was held by Lincoln since his earliest days. To the greater question of Christianity, Browning admitted, "To what extent he believed in the revelations and miracles of the Bible and New Testament, or whether he believed in them at all, I am not prepared to say; but I do know that he was not a scoffer at religion. During our long and intimate acquaintance and intercourse, I have no recollection of ever hearing an irreverent word fall from his lips."[67]

According to Wayne Temple, the best testimony is from John Hay and John Nicolay, who gave a brief mention of Lincoln's religion in their mammoth ten-volume work. Temple states that the two biographers "revealed that he 'was a man of profound and

intense religious feeling.' 'We have no purpose of attempting to for-
mulate his creed,' they confessed; 'we question if he himself ever
did so.' One could easily argue that they were exactly correct in
their analysis of this difficult matter." Nicolay had told Herndon
that Lincoln's beliefs had not changed in the White House, but on
the beliefs themselves he and Hay are on solid ground.[68]

OTHERS CLAIMED TO HAVE BEEN privy to information that showed
Lincoln was an orthodox Christian, but these claims generally defy
belief. For example, Mariah Vance, a maid in the Lincoln home
in Springfield, supposedly said that Lincoln was baptized, but this
has subsequently been shown to be groundless. General Daniel
Sickles said that Lincoln was converted after the battle of
Gettysburg and gave a long recollection of Lincoln explaining it to
him. However, Sickles was not a trustworthy figure and the supposed speech is very unlike those Lincoln gave elsewhere.[69]

Lincoln carried the religious habit of reading and studying the
Bible from Illinois to the White House. The clearest instance of
this was when in the summer of 1864, an African-American delegation from Baltimore gave him a beautiful Bible, bound in royal
purple velvet and with gold clasps and gold plates attached. This
gift had been paid for by donations from the African-American
community to thank him for his work on emancipation. Lincoln
thanked them, and then as one scholar recounts, "Coming to the
Bible itself, Lincoln said that everything the Lord gave the world
was 'communicated' through it; without it men would not know
right from wrong. . . . He referred to the Bible as 'the best gift God
has given to man.'" Lincoln was being politic to some extent at the
presentation of the gift, and exaggerated somewhat when he said
that without the Bible people could not know "right from
wrong."[70]

Lincoln's sentiments were heartfelt when he described the Bible as "the best gift" from God, however. Three telling incidents that same year show how much Lincoln studied and enjoyed the Bible. When a group of Republicans, dissatisfied with Lincoln, nominated their own candidate, John C. Frémont, for President in 1864, it was a disaster. Supposedly thousands were to attend their convention; a mere four hundred showed up. When hearing this number, Lincoln's thoughts immediately turned to the Bible. He reached for his and read to his listeners a passage from the Old Testament: "And every one who was in distress, and every one who was in debt, and every one who was discontented, gathered themselves unto him; and he became a captain over them: and there were with him about four hundred men" (1 Samuel 22:2).[71]

The second incident had Lincoln recalling an episode that happened when he was in school in Indiana. Seeing three members of the Senate who often gave him trouble coming over to the White House, Lincoln turned to a Senator standing next to him and told him a story. When he was a young boy, the students would line up and read passages from the Bible. This particular reading was about the three Hebrew children who were thrown in the fire but miraculously did not burn. One little boy had to read the three names. According to Lincoln, "He made a sorry mess of Shadrach and Meshach, and went all to pieces on Abednego." Since the old schools believed in "hands on" discipline, the boy had his ears boxed. The boy's crying turned to screams when he saw what his next turn to read would be. When the teacher demanded to know why he screamed, he answered, "there comes them same damn three fellows again!" Lincoln told the Senator that is how he felt when he saw his three constant critics coming toward the White House.[72]

The final example is Lincoln going back to an Old Testament story as reason for giving someone a second chance. A political

associate remembered Lincoln appointed a judge who was supposedly opposed to Lincoln's renomination for President. When
apprised of this, Lincoln replied that he had "scriptural reasons"
for giving the man the job. He continued, "When Moses was on
Mount Sinai, getting a commission for Aaron, that same Aaron was
at the foot of the mountain making a false god for the people to
worship. Yet Aaron got the commission."[73]

As Lincoln was set to begin his second term, his faith was never
stronger. The principles he had first become convinced of in
Springfield almost fifteen years before had been strengthened and
deepened by the war. As he prepared take his oath of office for
another four years, these thoughts were much on Lincoln's mind.
When it came time to write a speech for the occasion, Lincoln
would view the matter of the country and his experience as
President mainly in terms of Christian faith and scripture.

Chapter 6

THE SECOND
INAUGURATION

Woe unto the world because of offences!
—*Abraham Lincoln, "Second Inaugural Address," March 4, 1865*

L INCOLN SAT SILENTLY WITH HIS eyes closed pretending to be thinking of something other than what was going on in front of him. He was mortified. The man soon to be sworn in as his Vice-President was making a drunken spectacle of himself. Andrew Johnson had been added to the ticket in 1864 because he was from Tennessee, hoping to make the ticket truly national. A Democratic Senator who had courageously stayed loyal to the Union, Johnson was also supposed to win over Democrats who supported the war. Those ideas seemed far away on this day, as many in the Senate Chamber started whispering at the embarrassing nature of his speech.[1]

Johnson had a fever, and to fortify himself for his speech he took a drink of whiskey. This, unfortunately, led him to take a few more. Now he was intoxicated. What was supposed to be a seven-minute speech had gone on for seventeen. The outgoing Vice-President pulled at Johnson's coat-tails to make him stop. When it was finally over, Chief Justice Chase gave him the oath of office, after which Johnson grabbed the Bible, held it up, and kissed it, shouting, "I kiss this Book in the face of my nation of the United States." As the party made its way outside to hear Lincoln's Second Inaugural Address, Lincoln turned to one of the marshals of the ceremony and said quietly, "Do not let Johnson speak outside."[2]

It was an inauspicious beginning to the ceremonies. The overcast and chilly weather wasn't helpful either as Lincoln made his way outside on March 4, 1865. One might suspect that this would be a time for a little bit of crowing. The Democrats' candidate, General George B. McClellan, had failed utterly in his effort to gain enough votes among the rank and file of the army to secure his election. The troops still favored "Father Abraham." Lincoln had won reelection and the Confederate armies were on their last legs, yet a feeling of personal vindication was the most distant thing from Lincoln's mind. Lincoln had prepared a speech he thought America needed to hear.[3]

Lincoln's Second Inaugural Address, often considered Lincoln's greatest, deserves special attention because of its deeply religious nature. It was given only six weeks before Lincoln's death, making it his last major testimony on the subject. An inaugural address would usually be the last place to look for a president's personal religious views, yet here Lincoln offers insight into his thoughts at the time. He also makes explicit how his Christianity would affect his policy.

As he stepped out of the Senate Chamber, a thunderous applause arose. The band played "Hail to the Chief." Lincoln walked to the white iron table that had been put there by the Commissioner of Public Buildings. His speech had been set in type to read. He took out his eyeglasses and put them on as he held the address. He once joked years earlier that he needed glasses because he was "no longer a young man." That was even truer

Lincoln reads his second inaugural address on March 4, 1865. Lincoln is standing in the center of the photograph on the left side of the latticed balcony (*Library of Congress*)

now, after the war had taken its huge physical toll on him. As Lincoln started speak, the clouds cleared and the sun shone through. Noah Brooks, who was in the audience, later remembered, "The inaugural address was received in most profound silence. Every word was clear and audible as the ringing and somewhat shrill tones of Lincoln's voice sounded over the vast concourse."[4]

Lincoln then read what one scholar has called "The culmination of Lincoln's political faith." His speech began matter of factly, with an exposition of the current state of the union:

At this second appearing to take the oath of the presidential office, there is less occasion for an extended address than there was at the first. Then a statement, somewhat in detail, of a course to be pursued, seemed

> fitting and proper. Now, at the expiration of four years,
> during which public declarations have been constantly
> called forth on every point and phase of the great con-
> test which still absorbs the attention, and engrosses the
> energies of the nation, little that is new could be pre-
> sented. The progress of our arms, upon which all else
> chiefly depends, is as well known to the public as to
> myself; and it is, I trust, reasonably satisfactory and
> encouraging to all. With high hope for the future, no
> prediction in regard to it is ventured.[5]

Historian Ronald White has remarked on the oddness of the speech's opening, considering the event it was supposed to mark. "In these initial words Lincoln did not seem to build bridges to the aspirations of his Union audience. The audience was surely wait-ing to hear the re-elected president give voice to their feelings of victory, with the end of the war in sight. . . . After thirty-two years during which no president had been elected for a second term, Lincoln could only muster: '*At this second appearing*.'"[6]

Lincoln then continued with an exposition of the events that had occurred since his first inauguration:

> On the occasion corresponding to this four years ago,
> all thoughts were anxiously directed to an impending
> civil-war. All dreaded it—all sought to avert it. While
> the inaugural address was being delivered from this
> place, devoted altogether to saving the Union without
> war, insurgent agents were in the city seeking to destroy
> it without war—seeking to dissol[v]e the Union, and
> divide effects, by negotiation. Both parties deprecated
> war; but one of them would make war rather than let
> the nation survive; and the other would accept war
> rather than let it perish. And the war came.

The reference to "both parties" and the contrast between one who would "make war" and one who would "accept war" is a mild rebuke to the South. As one scholar put it, "Abraham Lincoln's refusal to claim the moral high ground exclusively for the North was even more extraordinary than his charity to a nearly defeated foe." Still, it is clear that, to Lincoln, "The North might not be perfect, but it clearly was on the side of the angels."[7]

Lincoln then moved into the main theme of his address. The third paragraph defined the heart of the war. Lincoln told the crowd:

> One eighth of the whole population were colored slaves, not distributed generally over the Union, but localized in the Southern part of it. These slaves constituted a peculiar and powerful interest. All knew that this interest was, somehow, the cause of the war. To strengthen, perpetuate, and extend this interest was the object for which the insurgents would rend the Union, even by war; while the government claimed no right to do more than to restrict the territorial enlargement of it. Neither party expected for the war, the magnitude, or the duration, which it has already attained. Neither anticipated that the cause of the conflict might cease with, or even before, the conflict itself should cease. Each looked for an easier triumph, and a result less fundamental and astounding. Both read the same Bible, and pray to the same God; and each invokes His aid against the other. It may seem strange that any men should dare to ask a just God's assistance in wringing their bread from the sweat of other men's faces; but let us judge not that we be not judged. The prayers of both could not be answered; that of neither has been

answered fully. The Almighty has His own purposes. "Woe unto the world because of offences! for it must needs be that offences come; but woe to that man by whom the offence cometh!" If we shall suppose that American Slavery is one of those offences which, in the providence of God, must needs come, but which, having continued through His appointed time, He now wills to remove, and that He gives to both North and South, this terrible war, as the woe due to those by whom the offence came, shall we discern therein any departure from those divine attributes which the believers in a Living God always ascribe to Him? Fondly do we hope—fervently do we pray—that this mighty scourge of war may speedily pass away. Yet, if God wills that it continue, until all the wealth piled by the bondman's two hundred and fifty years of unrequited toil shall be sunk, and until every drop of blood drawn with the lash, shall be paid by another drawn with the sword, as was said three thousand years ago, so still it must be said "the judgments of the Lord, are true and righteous altogether.[8]

Lincoln had taken the amazing step of explaining the war as the inevitable punishment that God had given the whole country for the sin of slavery. Lincoln quoted God's commandment to Adam after the fall. "In the sweat of thy face shalt thou eat bread, till thou return unto the ground; for out of it wast thou taken: for dust thou *art*, and unto dust shalt thou return" (Genesis 3:19). Slavery was nothing less than a breaking of that vital commandment. In referring to slavery Lincoln had used that biblical passage at least four times, starting in a speech he gave shortly before the war.[9]

Lincoln then invoked the Q passage that begins "Woe unto the world" and made the case for the war as divine punishment. On this point Lincoln differed with some of the leading theologians in America. They believed that America was exceptionally blessed by God. While Lincoln could speak of Americans as the "almost chosen people," he believed that America's sins in regards to slavery were as such to warrant the worst chastisement from God. One scholar has pictured Lincoln thinking back to the political heroes he had fought for, like Henry Clay. However, "Suddenly, those revered, distant, idealized figures lost their psychological significance. Lincoln had been lifted by history to look directly into the eyes of his heroes. It was a startling experience. And his gaze drifted upward. Finally only God, and no man, could supply the meaning of human existence."[10]

The famous close of the speech has perhaps overshadowed its grimmer aspects, but it is one of the classic examples of Lincoln's eloquence. He stated, "With malice toward none; with charity for all; with firmness in the right, as God gives us to see the right, let us strive on to finish the work we are in; to bind up the nation's wounds; to care for him who shall have borne the battle, and for his widow, and his orphan—to do all which may achieve and cherish a just, and a lasting peace, among ourselves, and with all nations." For Lincoln the necessity of forgiveness as it is taught in the Gospels was crucial.[11]

Historian Allen C. Guelzo sees a political edge to this closing. It attempted to answer the question "what now?" that most Americans were asking themselves. "The last paragraph of the address," Guelzo writes, "was Lincoln's answer, simple, supple in its last words, with grace of a benediction, as if he were once more miming the sermons of preachers to perfection. . . . One should move with firmness in the right, but with the caution that not every right we think we see is necessarily the right as God sees and reveals it...As inscrutability teaches a humility of ultimate intentions, so it teaches a humility of policy." A few weeks later Lincoln would put forward the policy more plainly when he told the officer in charge of occupied Richmond, "If I were in your place, I'd let 'em up easy, let 'em up easy."[12]

After Lincoln finished speaking, Chief Justice Salmon P. Chase administered the oath of office. Lincoln then kissed the open Bible. Chase, wanting to present the Bible to Mary Todd Lincoln as a gift, marked where Lincoln's lips had touched it, Isaiah 5:28-29, a passage that parallels Lincoln's speech. Isaiah there recounts how God will punish Israel for its sins, while Lincoln's address told of God's punishment of America for slavery.[13]

Failing to understand Lincoln as they had throughout the war, the Democratic newspapers were disgusted and bewildered by the speech. The *New York World*, perhaps the nation's leading Democratic paper, could say only, "Mr. Lincoln's substitution of religion for statesmanship is not less gratuitous than it is absurd. The President's theology smacks as strongly of the dark ages as does Pope Pius's politics." The *Detroit Free Press* said the speech "is more worthy of a puritanical hypocrite than of an American Executive." They failed to see that in Lincoln's mind the religious ideas made the statesmanship in this case. The forgiveness and humility preached by Christianity were the policies Lincoln's government would adopt.[14]

Foreign observers were taken aback by the theological nature of the speech. One Hebrew-language Romanian newspaper showed its shock as it told its readers, "One rather imagines himself transported into a camp of contrite sinners determined to leave the world and its vanities behind them, possessed of no other thought but that of reconciliation with their God, and addressed by their leader when about to set out on a course of penance." To the present day, Europe has viewed America's religiosity with some trepidation. However, the speech was not an exposition of God favoring America over others, and its humble tone was not threatening.[15]

The British reaction was genuinely favorable. Much of the British press had been hostile to Lincoln during the war. It had been, as it still is, great sport for British publications to poke fun of rude, country bumpkin Americans. The rail-splitter's appearance made an easy target and probably reinforced notions of a violent and uncivilized nation in America. Yet the speech was lauded in the British press. *The Spectator* said, "No statesman ever uttered words stamped at once with the seal of so deep a wisdom and so true a simplicity." The Duke of Argyll wrote his friend Senator Charles Sumner, "I . . . congratulate you both on the good progress of the war, and on the *remarkable speech* of your President. It was a noble speech, just and true, and solemn. I think it has produced a great effect in England."[16]

Many years later one British observer was also not deaf to the theological overtones of the speech. Lord Charnwood understood Lincoln better than most of America did. A genuine liberal, writing at the time of World War I, Charnwood said in admiration of the American President: "This man had stood alone in the dark. He had done justice; he had loved mercy; he had walked humbly with his God. The reader to whom religious utterances make little appeal will not suppose that his imaginative words stand for no real experience. The reader whose piety knows no questions will not be pained to think this man had professed no faith."[17]

About ten days after the address, Lincoln wrote a reply to what he thought was a compliment of his speech; though in reality the praise was for another piece. Lincoln thanked New York Republican boss Thurlow Weed for his "compliment." Lincoln again affirmed the theological ideas in the speech when he wrote, "Men are not flattered by being shown that there has been a difference of purpose between the Almighty and them. To deny it, however, in this case, is to deny that there is a God governing the world. It is a truth which I thought needed to be told; and as whatever of humiliation there is in it, falls most directly on myself, I thought others might afford for me to tell it."[18]

One person in the audience walked away from the speech disgusted. He too believed that God had intervened in America's history. A few months previously he had written, "This country was formed for the *white*, not for the black man. And looking upon *African slavery* from the same stand-point held by those noble framers of the Constitution, I for one have ever considered *it* one of the greatest blessings (both for themselves and us) that God ever bestowed upon a favored nation." Now after hearing Lincoln call slavery a sin that had been duly punished by God, John Wilkes Booth, who had signed the above statement, "A *Confederate, doing duty upon his own responsibility*," was more than ever convinced that something drastic needed to be done.[19]

CONCLUSION

T HE TRAGIC CODA OF ABRAHAM LINCOLN'S life is known to
everyone. At his moment of triumph, he was taken. He was
shot on Good Friday, a day commemorating the violent death of a
man he so admired. American history was forever changed; with
Andrew Johnson in the White House, any racial justice was put off
for decades. Had Lincoln lived, things would have gone better;
they couldn't have gone worse. In any case, the country mourned
its fallen chief. His death touched the freed slaves maybe more
than the rest of the country because they sensed they lost a friend.[1]

The funeral in the White House was impressive and solemn.
Reverend Thomas Hall, pastor of the Epiphany Episcopal Church
in Washington, was the first to speak on that somber April 19, as
Lincoln lay in state. Rev. Gurley officiated, but several denominations were present. From the Gospel of John, Hall read the opening of the Episcopal funeral service, "I am the Resurrection, and
the life; he that believeth in me, though he were dead, yet shall he
live. And whosoever liveth and believeth in me shall never die"
(John 11:25-26). Across America, churches were turning to the
same text for comfort.[2]

153

Later, as the funeral train made its way across America, the Lincoln legend was being born. By the time his body was placed in a temporary crypt in May, the lines of conflict over his religion were already being drawn. They continue to the present day. On one side ranged Herndon, Lamon, Ingersoll, and the others who said Lincoln was an infidel in his youth and remained one till the day of his death. On the other side were men like Holland, Brooks, and Smith, who believed whatever Lincoln's beliefs were when he was young, he was a believer in the orthodox Christian faith when he died.

Defining Lincoln as an infidel or an orthodox Christian leaves out other possibilities. This limitation led Mary Todd Lincoln to tell Herndon her husband was not a "technical Christian." It also led the freethinker Robert Ingersoll to post his seven basic conditions of being a Christian to prove Lincoln couldn't pass all of them. The last of those requirements was "He believes in the Trinity, in God the Father, God the Son and God the Holy Ghost."[3]

Lincoln was neither an infidel nor an orthodox Christian. He believed in the wisdom and the atoning death of Jesus, but did not necessarily believe Jesus was equal to God. Lincoln was also familiar with the original teachings of Christ through the Q material in the Gospels of Matthew and Luke, and tried to live according to them. Herndon saw this and was moved to write, "Do you not see Lincoln's Christ like charity—liberality—toleration loom up & blossom above all?" Similarly, Herndon remembered Lincoln liked the old Unitarian quote, "When I do good I feel good, when I do bad I feel bad, and that's my religion."[4] These views harkened back to a primitive form of Christianity that is no longer seen as a viable option today. Lincoln's religious thought was closer to the historical Jesus and the earliest Christianity than many orthodox Christians of his day were. Many early Christians saw Jesus as Lord and whose death and resurrection placed him high above the rest of humanity, but not necessarily on the same plane as God. They were still fiercely monotheistic. Lincoln viewed God and Christ the same way they did. Over the course of the first several centuries of Christianity, this proto-orthodox view became the minority, and orthodox views, which included the concept of God as a Trinity, became established. Lincoln's beliefs never went along with these changes.

My effort in this book has been to examine in detail the available evidence about Abraham Lincoln's religious beliefs as a way to explore an individual's dialogue with religion over the course of a lifetime. Beyond its intrinsic appeal, this inquiry demonstrates that decisions about good government based on a fixed idea of a person's religious faith are not relevant to who does or does not possess the skills to be a leader, even a great leader.

Perhaps Lincoln's Christianity is best captured in his explanation why he never formally joined a church:

> I have never united myself to any church, because I have found it difficult in giving my assent, without mental reservation, to the long, complicated statements of Christian doctrine which characterize their Articles of Faith. When any church will inscribe over its altar, as its sole qualification for membership, the Saviour's condensed statement of the substance of both Law and Gospel, "Thou shalt love the Lord thy God with all thy heart, and with all thy soul, and with all thy mind, and thy neighbor as thyself," that church will I join with all my heart and all my soul.[5]

NOTES

Introduction: The Question of Lincoln's Faith

[1] Paul C. Nagel, *Descent from Glory: Four Generations of the John Adams Family* (New York: Oxford University Press, 1983), 128.

[2] Benjamin P. Thomas, *Portrait for Posterity: Lincoln and His Biographers* (New Brunswick: Rutgers University Press, 1947), 3-4; Josiah G. Holland, *The Life of Abraham Lincoln* (Springfield, Mass.: Samuel Bowles and Company, 1866); Ward Hill Lamon, *The Life of Abraham Lincoln: From His Birth to His Inauguration as President* (Lincoln: University of Nebraska Press, 1999).

[3] William J. Wolf, *The Almost Chosen People: A Study of the Religion of Abraham Lincoln* (Garden City, N.Y.: Doubleday, 1959); David Elton Trueblood, *Abraham Lincoln: Theologian of American Anguish* (New York: Harper & Row, 1973).

[4] Abraham Lincoln as quoted in Reinhard H. Luthin, *The Real Abraham Lincoln: A Complete One Volume History of His Life and Times* (Englewood Cliffs: Prentice-Hall, 1960), xi.

[5] Bernard Von Bothmer, "Devout Believer or Skeptic Politician? An Overview of Historians' Analyses of Abraham Lincoln's Religion: 1859-2001," *Lincoln Herald* 107, no. 4 (Winter 2005): 155.

[6] Russel Blaine Nye, *The Cultural Life of the New Nation: 1776-1830* (New York: Harper & Row, 1963), 216-218.

[7] David Herbert Donald, *Lincoln Reconsidered: Essays on the Civil War Era* (New York: Vintage Books, 1989), 3-15; Abraham Lincoln to the Editor of the *Sangamo Journal*, June 13, 1836, in Roy P. Basler, Marion Dolores Pratt, and Lloyd A. Dunlap, eds., *The Collected Works of Abraham Lincoln*, 8 vols. and index (New Brunswick: Rutgers University Press, 1953), 1:48.

[8] John Hay to William Herndon, September 5, 1866, in Michael Burlingame, ed., *At Lincoln's Side: John Hay's Civil War Correspondence and Selected Writings* (Carbondale: Southern Illinois University Press, 2000), 111.

[9] Lincoln's parents possessed an English translation of the older Geneva Bible, which is now owned by the National Park Service.

Chapter 1: Frontier Religion

[1] Matthew Pinkser, *Lincoln's Sanctuary: Abraham Lincoln and the Soldier's Home* (Oxford: Oxford University Press, 2003), 151; David Herbert Donald, *"We Are Lincoln Men": Abraham Lincoln and His Friends* (New York: Simon & Schuster, 2003), 46, 63. I find Donald's doubt of this episode unpersuasive. The story is not likely to be a pious forgery by Speed, for nowhere does he claim to be convinced of Lincoln's wisdom on this matter. Also, the fact that the wealthy Speed left a bequest to a Methodist church seems like run-of-the-mill philanthropy, similar to the atheist/agnostic Andrew Carnegie leaving money for church organs.

[2] Mary Todd Lincoln, September 1866, in Douglas L. Wilson and Rodney O. Davis, eds., *Herndon's Informants: Letters, Interviews, and Statements About Abraham Lincoln* (Urbana: University of Illinois Press, 1998), 360.

[3] Mark E. Neely, Jr., *The Abraham Lincoln Encyclopedia* (New York: Da Capo Press, 1982), 260; Louis A. Warren, *Lincoln's Parentage and Childhood: A History of the Kentucky Lincolns Supported by Documentary*

Evidence (New York: Century, 1926), 233-234.

4 Wolf, *Almost Chosen People*, 37.

5 Ibid., 37; John T. Morse as quoted in William E. Barton, *The Soul of Abraham Lincoln* (New York: George H. Doran, 1920), 44-45; Don E. Fehrenbacher and Virginia Fehrenbacher, eds., *Recollected Words of Abraham Lincoln* (Stanford: Stanford University Press, 1996), 372.

6 William H. Herndon and Jesse W. Weik, *Herndon's Life of Lincoln* (New York: Da Capo Press, 1983), 15, 480; Barton, *Soul of Abraham Lincoln*, 63.

7 William E. Barton, *The Life of Abraham Lincoln*, 2 vols. (Indianapolis: Bobbs-Merrill Company, 1925), 1:107; Allen C. Guelzo, "Abraham Lincoln and the Doctrine of Necessity," *Journal of the Abraham Lincoln Association* 18, no. 1 (Winter 1997), 67; Gordon Leidner, *Lincoln on God and Country* (Shippensburg, Pa.: White Mane Publishing, 2000), 5.

8 Nancy Hanks Lincoln as quoted in Herndon and Weik, *Herndon's Life of Lincoln*, 27; John Johnston to Abraham Lincoln as quoted in Kenneth J. Winkle, *The Young Eagle: The Rise of Abraham Lincoln* (Dallas: Taylor Trade Publishing, 2001), 144, 145.

9 Abraham Lincoln, "Copybook Verses," in Basler et al., *Collected Works*, 1:1; Barton, *Soul of Abraham Lincoln*, 49.

10 Abraham Lincoln, "Copybook Verses," in Basler et al., *Collected Works*, 1:1.

11 Louis A. Warren, *Lincoln's Youth: The Indiana Years, Seven to Twenty-one, 1816-1830* (Indianapolis: Indiana Historical Society, 1991), 121, 115; Matilda Johnston Moore to William Herndon, September 8, 1866, in Wilson and Davis, *Herndon's Informants*, 110; Warren, 121; Ida M. Tarbell, *In the Footsteps of the Lincolns* (New York: Harper and Brothers, 1924), 145.

12 Dennis F. Hanks to William Herndon, June 13, 1865, in *Herndon's Informants*, 39, 41. Abraham Lincoln to Jesse W. Fell, December 20, 1859, in Basler et al., *Collected Works*, 3:511.

13 Abraham Lincoln as quoted in Douglas L. Wilson, *Honor's Voice: The Transformation of Abraham Lincoln* (New York: Knopf, 1998), 301; Abraham Lincoln as quoted in Michael Burlingame, *The Inner World of Abraham Lincoln* (Urbana: University of Illinois Press, 1994), 150; Tarbell, *In the Footsteps of the Lincolns*, 270-271.

14 P. M. Zall, ed., *Abe Lincoln Laughing: Humorous Anecdotes from Original Sources by and About Abraham Lincoln* (Knoxville: University of Tennessee Press, 1997), 53.

15 Ibid., 112; Abraham Lincoln to Mary Owens, May 7, 1837, in Basler et al., *Collected Works*, 1:78.

16 Orville H. Browning to Isaac A. Arnold, 1872, in Michael Burlingame, ed., *An Oral History of Abraham Lincoln: John G. Nicolay's Interviews and Essays* (Carbondale: Southern Illinois University Press, 1996), 130; Orville H. Browning to John G. Nicolay, June 17, 1875, in ibid., 5.

17 Wilson and Davis, *Herndon's Informants*, 744; Elizabeth Crawford to William Herndon, February 21, 1866, in ibid., 215.

18 Dennis F. Hanks to William H. Herndon, May 19, 1866, in ibid., 233; Sarah Bush Lincoln, September 8, 1866, in ibid., 107, 108.

19 David Herbert Donald, *Lincoln* (New York: Simon & Schuster, 1995), 35; Herndon and Weik, *Herndon's Life of Lincoln*, 45; Donald, 35.

20 Joshua F. Speed, *Reminiscences of Abraham Lincoln and Notes of a Visit to California: Two Lectures* (Louisville: John P. Morton, 1884), 17-18; Abraham Lincoln as quoted in ibid., 18; Abraham Lincoln, "Temperance Address," February 22, 1842, in Basler et al., *Collected Works*, 1:274-275.

21 Donald, *Lincoln*, 15; Wayne C. Temple, *Abraham Lincoln: From Skeptic to Prophet* (Mahomet: Mayhaven Publishing, 1995), 17; Mary Todd Lincoln, September 1866, in Wilson and Davis, *Herndon's Informants*, 358; Joseph Gillespie to William Herndon, December 8, 1866, in ibid., 506; William Herndon to Jesse Weik, February 26, 1891, in Emmanuel Hertz, ed., *The Hidden Lincoln: From the Letters and Papers of William H. Herndon* (Garden City, N.Y.: Blue Ribbon Books, 1938), 265.

[22] Donald, *Lincoln*, 15; Abraham Lincoln, Speech at Peoria, Illinois, October 4, 1854, in Basler et al., *Collected Works*, 2:255.

[23] Winkle, *The Young Eagle*, 1-2; William E. Barton, *The Lineage of Lincoln* (Indianapolis: Bobbs-Merrill Company, 1929), 28; Joseph R. Fornieri, *Abraham Lincoln's Political Faith* (DeKalb: Northern Illinois University Press, 2003), 25.

[24] Edmund S. Morgan, *The Puritan Dilemma: The Story of John Winthrop* (New York: Harper Collins, 1958), 7-8.

[25] William Herndon as quoted in Allen C. Guelzo, *Abraham Lincoln: Redeemer President* (Grand Rapids: William B. Eerdmans, 1999), 118.

[26] David Herbert Donald, *Lincoln's Herndon: A Biography* (New York: Da Capo Press, 1989), 359; William Herndon to Ward Hill Lamon, March 6, 1870 in Hertz, *Hidden Lincoln*, 78.

[27] Guelzo, *Redeemer President*, 117-121.

[28] Robert G. Ingersoll, "The Gentlest Memory of Our World," in *Reminiscences of Abraham Lincoln by Distinguished Men of His Time*, ed. Allen Thorndike Rice (New York: Harper and Brothers, 1909), 424.

[29] Dumas Malone and Basil Rauch, *Empire for Liberty: The Genesis and Growth of the United States of America*, 2 vols. (New York: Appleton-Century-Crofts, 1960), 1:509; David Zarefsky, *Lincoln, Douglas, and Slavery: In the Crucible of Public Debate* (Chicago: University of Chicago Press, 1990), 18.

[30] Nathaniel Grigsby to William Herndon, January 21, 1866, in Wilson and Davis, *Herndon's Informants*, 169; Abraham Lincoln, "Communication to the People of Sangamo County," March 9, 1832, in Basler et al., *Collected Works*, 1:8.

[31] Joshua F. Speed to William Herndon, November 30, 1866, in Wilson and Davis, *Herndon's Informants*, 430.

[32] Douglas L. Wilson, *Lincoln Before Washington: New Perspectives on the Illinois Years* (Urbana: University of Illinois Press, 1997), 98-132; Abraham Lincoln to Joshua F. Speed, July 4, 1842, in Basler et al., *Collected Works*, 1:289.

33 Abraham Lincoln to Mary Speed, September, 27, 1841 in Basler et al., *Collected Works*, 1:261.

34 Thomas Paine as quoted in Robert J. Havlick, "Some Influences of Thomas Paine's 'Age of Reason' upon Abraham Lincoln," *Lincoln Herald* 104, no. 2 (Summer 2002), 66; Abraham Lincoln, "Campaign Circular from Whig Committee," March 4, 1843, in Basler et al., *Collected Works*, 1:315.

Chapter 2: The Young Skeptic

1 Benjamin P. Thomas, *Lincoln's New Salem* (Carbondale: Southern Illinois University Press, 1987), 59-61.

2 Barton, *Life of Abraham Lincoln*, 1:192-201; Thomas P. Reep, *Lincoln at New Salem* (Petersburg, Ill.: Old Salem Lincoln League, 1927), 53-54; Guelzo, *Redeemer President*, 49.

3 James Short as quoted in Guelzo, *Redeemer President*, 49; Albert J. Beveridge, *Abraham Lincoln: 1809-1858*, 2 vols. (Boston: Houghton Mifflin, 1928), 1:135; Mentor Graham to William Herndon, July 15, 1865, in Wilson and Davis, *Herndon's Informants*, 76.

4 Donald, *Lincoln*, 49; Beveridge, *Abraham Lincoln*, 1:139; Volney as quoted in Beveridge, 1:139; Walter B. Stevens, *A Reporter's Lincoln* (Lincoln: University of Nebraska Press, 1998), 11-12.

5 Wolf, *Almost Chosen People*, 45.

6 John Hill, "A Romance of Reality," February 15, 1862, in Wilson and Davis, *Herndon's Informants*, 25, 24.

7 Wolf, *Almost Chosen People*, 46-47.

8 Isaac Cogdal in Wilson and Davis, *Herndon's Informants*, 441; William Herndon as quoted in Lamon, *Life of Abraham Lincoln*, 489.

9 See Daniel Walker Howe, *The Political Culture of American Whigs* (Chicago: University of Chicago Press, 1979).

10 Donald W. Riddle, *Lincoln Runs for Congress* (New Brunswick: Rutgers University Press, 1948), 173; Dr. Boal to Richard Yates, August 25, 1860, as quoted in ibid., 173.

[11] Abraham Lincoln, "Handbill Replying to Charges of Infidelity," July 31, 1846 in Basler et al., *Collected Works*, 1:382.

[12] Donald, *Lincoln*, 49.

[13] Stephen B. Oates, *Abraham Lincoln: The Man Behind the Myths* (New York: HarperPerennial, 1984), 53.

[14] Neely, *Abraham Lincoln Encyclopedia*, 292.

[15] Benjamin P. Thomas, *Abraham Lincoln: A Biography* (New York: Modern Library, 1968), 43; John Todd Stuart as quoted in Paul Simon, *Lincoln's Preparation for Greatness: The Illinois Legislature Years* (Urbana: University of Illinois Press, 1971), 16; Thomas, *Abraham Lincoln*, 42-43.

[16] Wilson, *Honor's Voice*, 233-264; Abraham Lincoln to John T. Stuart, January 23, 1841, in Basler et al., *Collected Works*, 1:229, 230.

[17] John T. Stuart, December 20, 1866, in Wilson and Davis, *Herndon's Informants*, 519; John T. Stuart, March 2, 1870, in ibid., 576.

[18] Neely, *Abraham Lincoln Encyclopedia*, 207.

[19] James H. Matheny in Wilson and Davis, *Herndon's Informants*, 432.

[20] Ibid., 472, 576-577.

[21] William Baringer, *Lincoln's Rise to Power* (Boston: Little, Brown, 1937), 128, 267; Herndon and Weik, *Herndon's Life of Lincoln*, 357-359; Jesse W. Fell to Ward Hill Lamon, September 22, 1870, in Wilson and Davis, *Herndon's Informants*, 579-580.

[22] Wolf, *Almost Chosen People*, 106-107.

[23] Abraham Lincoln, "Speech in the U.S. House of Representatives on the Presidential Question," July 27, 1848, in Basler et al., *Collected Works*, 1:503.

[24] Lamon, *Life of Abraham Lincoln*, 504; William Herndon to Charles H. Hart, December 28, 1866, in Hertz, *Hidden Lincoln*, 52.

[25] Guelzo, *Redeemer President*, 20.

[26] Jesse W. Weik, *The Real Lincoln: A Portrait* (Boston: Houghton Mifflin, 1922), 112; Charles B. Strozier, *Lincoln's Quest for Union: Public and Private Meanings* (New York: Basic Books, 1982), 205.

27 Robert V. Bruce, "The Riddle of Death," in *The Lincoln Enigma: The Changing Face of an American Icon*, ed. Gabor S. Boritt (New York: Oxford University Press, 2001), 137; Burlingame, *Inner World of Abraham Lincoln*, 93-94; for an excellent look at Lincoln's depression see Burlingame, 92-122.

28 John Evangelist Walsh, *The Shadows Rise: Abraham Lincoln and the Ann Rutledge Legend* (Urbana: University of Illinois Press, 1993), 63, 121; for the controversy on this incident see Michael Burkhimer, *100 Essential Lincoln Books* (Nashville: Cumberland House, 2003), 92, 240-242.

29 Bruce, "Riddle of Death," 134-135; Abraham Lincoln to Andrew Johnson, April 18, 1846, in Basler et al., *Collected Works*, 1:378; Abraham Lincoln, "Eulogy on Zachary Taylor," July 25, 1850 in ibid., 2:90; Ward Hill Lamon, *Recollections of Abraham Lincoln: 1847-1865* (Lincoln: University of Nebraska Press, 1995), 155; Francis B. Carpenter, *The Inner Life of Abraham Lincoln: Six Months in the White House* (Lincoln: University of Nebraska Press, 1995), 60; William Knox, "Mortality" in ibid., 60-61.

30 Herndon and Weik, *Herndon's Life of Lincoln*, 258; Oliver Wendell Holmes, "The Last Leaf," as quoted in Burlingame, *Inner World of Abraham Lincoln*, 113.

31 Neely, *Abraham Lincoln Encyclopedia*, 240; Abraham Lincoln, "Memoranda on Robert Burns," January 25, 1865, in Basler et al., *Collected Works*, 8:237.

32 "Holy Willie's Prayer," in Robert Burns, *Robert Burns: Selected Poems* (New York: Penguin Books, 1993), 20-22.

33 Abraham Lincoln, "My Childhood-Home I See Again," February 25, 1846, in Basler et al., *Collected Works*, 1:367.

34 Abraham Lincoln to Andrew Johnston, September 6, 1846, in ibid., 1:386.

35 Joshua Wolf Shenk, *Lincoln's Melancholy: How Depression Challenged a President and Fueled His Greatness* (Boston: Houghton

Mifflin, 2005), 39; Joshua F. Speed in Wilson and Davis, *Herndon's Informants*, 30; Joshua F. Speed to William Herndon, September 13, 1866, in ibid., 337; William Herndon to Ward Hill Lamon, February 25, 1870, in Hertz, *Hidden Lincoln*, 67; Robert S. Harper, *Lincoln and the Press* (New York: McGraw-Hill, 1951), 2.

36 Shenk, *Lincoln's Melancholy*, 39.

37 "A Suicide's Soliloquy" as quoted in Richard Lawrence Miller, "Lincoln's Suicide Poem: Has It Been Found?" *For the People* 6, no. 1 (Spring 2004), 6.

38 Shenk, *Lincoln's Melancholy*, 41.

39 Guelzo, *Redeemer President*, 50; Abraham Lincoln as quoted in Henry B. Rankin, *Personal Recollections of Abraham Lincoln* (New York: G. P. Putnam's Sons, 1916), 326.

Chapter 3: Reverend Smith's Book

1 Herndon and Weik, *Herndon's Life of Lincoln*, 36; Temple, *From Skeptic to Prophet*, 37-39.

2 Herndon and Weik, *Herndon's Life of Lincoln*, 36; Ruth Painter Randall, *Mary Lincoln: Biography of a Marriage* (Boston: Little, Brown, 1953), 73; Jennifer Fleischner, *Mrs. Lincoln and Mrs. Keckly: The Remarkable Story of the Friendship Between a First Lady and a Former Slave* (New York: Broadway Books, 2003), 151; John P. Frank, *Lincoln as a Lawyer* (Chicago: Americana House, 1991), 31-36; Temple, *From Skeptic to Prophet*, 37.

3 Temple, *From Skeptic to Prophet*, 37-38; James Smith, *The Christian's Defence, Containing a Fair Statement, and Impartial Examination of the Leading Objections Urged by Infidels Against the Antiquity, Genuineness, Credibility and Inspiration of the Holy Scriptures*, 2 vols. in 1 (Cincinnati: J. A. James, 1843), ix-x.

4 Temple, *From Skeptic to Prophet*, 38.

5 Barton, *Soul of Abraham Lincoln*, 358; Smith, *Christian's Defence*, x.

6 Barton, *Soul of Abraham Lincoln*, 358.

7 Temple, *From Skeptic to Prophet*, 39; Edgar DeWitt Jones, *Lincoln and the Preachers* (Freeport: Harper & Brothers, 1948), 30; Lincoln's "skinning of Thomas" was an example of this sarcastic and belittling tone he could adopt on the stump, an episode related in Herndon and Weik, *Herndon's Life of Lincoln*, 159; "Southwestern Christian Advocate," 1841, as quoted in Barton, *Soul of Abraham Lincoln*, 360-361.

8 Members of the Methodist Church to James Smith, May 1, 1841, as quoted in Smith, *Christian's Defence*, xi.

9 Barton, *Soul of Abraham Lincoln*, 158; Earl Schenk Miers, ed., *Lincoln Day by Day: A Chronology, 1809-1865*, 3 vols. in 1 (Dayton: Morningside, 1991), 2:24; Thomas Lewis, January 6, 1873, as quoted in Barton, 163.

10 Abraham Lincoln, "Temperance Address," February 22, 1842, in Basler et al., *Collected Works*, 1:279; Smith, *Christian's Defence*, 1:3-4.

11 Smith, *Christian's Defence*, 1:105.

12 James W. Keyes, in Wilson and Davis, *Herndon's Informants*, 464.

13 Smith, *Christian's Defence*, 1:99; Barton, *Soul of Abraham Lincoln*, 358.

14 Smith, *Christian's Defence*, 1:108, 110-116, 114; Abraham Lincoln, "First Debate with Stephen A. Douglas at Ottawa, Illinois," August 21, 1858, in Basler et al., *Collected Works*, 3:16.

15 Smith, *Christian's Defence*, 1:72-73.

16 Ibid., 1:73.

17 Ibid., 2:8-9.

18 Ibid., 2:82.

19 Ibid., 2:41-72.

20 Ibid., 2:8, 158-171.

21 Ibid., 2:131-132; Raymond E. Brown, *An Introduction to the New Testament* (New York: Doubleday, 1997), 172, 334-335.

22 Smith, *Christian's Defence*, 2:133; Abraham Lincoln, "Address Before the Young Men's Lyceum of Springfield, Illinois," January 27, 1838, in Basler et al., *Collected Works*, 1:115.

23 Thomas Paine as quoted in Havlick, "Some Influences of Thomas Paine's Age of Reason Upon Abraham Lincoln," 64-65.

24 Smith, *Christian's Defence*, 2:301.

25 Ibid., 2:318, 322, 324.

26 Ibid., 2:358-359.

27 Ninian Wirt Edwards, December 24, 1872, as quoted in Barton, *Soul of Abraham Lincoln*, 164.

28 Jean H. Baker, *Mary Todd Lincoln: A Biography* (New York: W. W. Norton, 1987), 125-126; Lloyd Ostendorf, *Lincoln's Photographs: A Complete Album* (Dayton: Rockywood Press, 1998), 364-365; Roger Norton, "Eddie Lincoln," *Abraham Lincoln Research Site*. http://home.att.net/~rjnorton/Lincoln67.html (accessed April 20, 2007); Fleischner, *Mrs. Lincoln and Mrs. Keckly*, 169.

29 Wayne C. Temple, *By Square and Compasses: The Building of the Lincoln Home and Its Saga* (Bloomington: Ashler Press, 1984), 11; Baker, *Mary Todd Lincoln*, 126; Jason Emerson, "'Of Such Is the Kingdom of Heaven'": The Mystery of 'Little Eddie,'" *Journal of the Illinois State Historical Society* (Autumn 1999) http://www.findarticles.com/p/articles/mi_qa3945/is_199910/ai_n8862405/ (accessed July 13, 2006).

30 John Todd Stuart to Rev. J. A. Reed, December 17, 1872, as quoted in Barton, *Soul of Abraham Lincoln*, 319-320; John T. Stuart, March 2, 1870, in Wilson and Davis, *Herndon's Informants*, 576.

31 James H. Matheny, March 6, 1870, in Wilson and Davis, *Herndon's Informants*, 577; Guelzo, *Redeemer President*, 158; James H. Matheny to Rev. J. A. Reed, December 16, 1872, as quoted in Barton, *Soul of Abraham Lincoln*, 321.

32 Merrill D. Peterson, *Lincoln in American Memory* (New York: Oxford University Press, 1994), 80; Lamon, *Life of Abraham Lincoln*, 486-504.

[33] William Herndon to Ward Hill Lamon, March 6, 1870, in Hertz, *Hidden Lincoln*, 77; Guelzo, *Redeemer President*, 157; Hertz, 78.

[34] Robert Todd Lincoln to William Herndon, December 24, 1866, in Wilson and Davis, *Herndon's Informants*, 524; John S. Goff, *Robert Todd Lincoln: A Man in His Own Right* (Norman: University of Oklahoma Press, 1969), 46-58.

[35] Mary Todd Lincoln to James Smith, June 8, 1870, in Turner and Turner, *Mary Todd Lincoln*, 567-568.

[36] Robert J. Havlick, "Abraham Lincoln and the Reverend Dr. James Smith: Lincoln's Presbyterian Experience of Springfield," *Journal of the Illinois Historical Society* (Autumn 1999) http://www.findarticles.com /p/articles/mi_qa3945/is_199910/ai_n8861124/ (accessed July 13, 2006); Trueblood, *Theologian of American Anguish*, 96; Temple, *From Skeptic to Prophet*, 50-51, 60. Lincoln's pew is now on display in front of the church in Springfield.

[37] James Smith to William Herndon, December 24, 1867, in Wilson and Davis, *Herndon's Informants*, 547-550.

[38] Ibid.

[39] Abraham Lincoln to John D. Johnston, January 12, 1851, in Basler et al., *Collected Works*, 2:97. The letter was faded and the editors have added the probable words in brackets; Donald, *Lincoln*, 153.

[40] William H. Hanna in Wilson and Davis, *Herndon's Informants*, 458.

[41] Lucas E. Morel, *Lincoln's Sacred Effort: Defining Religion's Role in American Self-Government* (Lanham, Md.: Lexington Books, 2000), 147; James Smith, as quoted in ibid., 148; ibid., 147.

[42] Ibid., 148; Abraham Lincoln, "An Address Delivered Before the Springfield Washington Temperance Society" February 22, 1842, in Basler et al., *Collected Works*, 1:272.

[43] Havlick, "Abraham Lincoln and the Reverend Dr. James Smith"; Abraham Lincoln, "First Lecture on Discoveries and Inventions," April 8, 1858, in Basler et al., *Collected Works*, 2:437-442.

[44] Temple, *From Skeptic to Prophet*, 55; Havlick, "Abraham Lincoln and the Reverend Dr. James Smith"; Mary Todd Lincoln to Emile Todd Helm, November 23, 1856, in Turner and Turner, *Mary Todd Lincoln*, 47.

[45] Jones, *Lincoln and the Preachers*, 34; Temple, *From Skeptic to Prophet*, 156, 159-160, 162, 161, 157.

[46] Walsh, *The Shadows Rise*, 79, 82-85.

[47] Wilson and Davis, *Herndon's Informants*, 757; Isaac Cogdal to B. F. Irwin, April 10, 1874, as quoted in Walsh, *The Shadows Rise*, 81-82; Isaac Cogdal in Wilson and Davis, 441.

[48] Wilson and Davis, *Herndon's Informants*, 776; John H. Wickizer to William Herndon, December 13, 1866, in ibid., 516; Richard J. Carwardine, "Lincoln, Evangelical Religion, and American Political Culture in the Era of the Civil War," *Journal of the Abraham Lincoln Association* 18, no. 1 (Winter 1997), 36.

[49] Temple, *From Skeptic to Prophet*, 67; Abraham Lincoln, "Speech at Kalamazoo, Michigan," August 27, 1856, in Basler et al., *Collected Works*, 2:366; Abraham Lincoln, "Fragments: Notes for Speeches," September 1859, in Basler et al., 3:399; Abraham Lincoln, "Speech at Clinton, Illinois," October 14, 1859, in Basler et al., 3:488.

[50] See Eric Foner, *Free Soil, Free Labor, Free Men: The Ideology of the Republican Party Before the Civil War* (New York: Oxford University Press, 1970).

[51] Abram J. Dittenhoefer, *How We Elected Lincoln: Personal Recollections* (Philadelphia: University of Pennsylvania Press, 2005), 39.

[52] Ibid., 41-42.

[53] Holland, *Life of Abraham Lincoln*, 236-237.

[54] Allen C. Guelzo, "Holland's Informants: The Construction of Josiah Holland's 'Life of Abraham Lincoln,'" *Journal of the Abraham Lincoln Association* 23, no. 1 (Winter 2002), 11.

[55] Holland, *Life of Abraham Lincoln*, 240; Guelzo, "Holland's Informants," 11; Thomas, *Portrait for Posterity*, 16.

[56] Newton Bateman to William Herndon, March 8, 1869, in Wilson and Davis, *Herndon's Informants*, 572; Isaac Arnold to William Herndon, December 18, 1882, in ibid., 588.

[57] Barton, *Soul of Abraham Lincoln*, 123-124.

[58] Abraham Lincoln, "Fragment on Pro-Slavery Theology," October 1, 1858, in Basler et al., *Collected Works*, 3:204.

[59] Barton, *Soul of Abraham Lincoln*, 127.

[60] Herndon and Weik, *Herndon's Life of Lincoln*, 387-388, 389.

[61] Richard Carwardine, *Lincoln: A Life of Purpose and Power* (New York: Knopf, 2006), 4.; James W. Keys in Wilson and Davis, *Herndon's Informants*, 464; Noyes Miner as quoted in Guelzo, *Redeemer President*, 116.

[62] Paul M. Angle, *Here I Have Lived: A History of Lincoln's Springfield* (Springfield: Abraham Lincoln Association, 1935), 260; Abraham Lincoln, "Farewell Address at Springfield Illinois," February 11, 1861, in Basler et al., *Collected Works*, 4:190. There are a number of versions of this speech. They do not differ materially in the points made. This version is the best-known one and was written out by Lincoln shortly after delivering it; James Conkling as quoted in William E. Baringer, *A House Dividing: Lincoln as President-Elect* (Springfield: Abraham Lincoln Association, 1945), 266; Victor Searcher, *Lincoln's Journey to Greatness: A Factual Account of the Twelve-Day Inaugural Trip* (Philadelphia: John C. Winston, 1960), 5.

Chapter 4: Early Christian Sources and Lincoln's Rhetoric

[1] Fawn M. Brodie, *Thomas Jefferson: An Intimate History* (New York: W. W. Norton, 1974), 371-374; Thomas Jefferson as quoted in ibid., 372.

[2] John P. Meier, *A Marginal Jew: Rethinking the Historical Jesus*, vol. 1: *The Roots of the Problem and the Person* (New York: Doubleday, 1991),

1:60-65. In the core part of the statement that was not the result of later Christian interpolations, Josephus is mistaken on one point when says that Jesus won over many of "Greek origin." Jesus' mission was in fact to the Jews. Josephus probably looked at the Christians of his day being mostly Gentiles, after the successful missionary work of Paul, Barnabas, Timothy, and others, and simply assumed Jesus would have had Gentile followers in his own lifetime.

[3] Robert Van Voorst, *Jesus Outside the New Testament: An Introduction to the Ancient Evidence* (Grand Rapids: William B. Eerdmans, 2000), 73-74.

[4] Abraham Lincoln to Lyman Trumbull, December 10, 1860, in Basler et al., *Collected Works*, 4:149-150.

[5] Ibid., 127, 172, 226, 334; Gerd Theissen and Annette Merz, *The Historical Jesus: A Comprehensive Guide*, translated by John Bowden (Minneapolis: Fortress Press, 1998), 25-36; E. P. Sanders, *The Historical Figure of Jesus* (London: Penguin Books, 1993), 64.

[6] Meier, *Marginal Jew*, 1:44; Paula Fredriksen, *Jesus of Nazareth: King of the Jews* (New York: Vintage Books, 1999), 33-34.

[7] G. K. Chesterton, *What's Wrong with the World?* (San Francisco: Ignatius Press, 1994), 21.

[8] Marcus Borg, *The Lost Gospel Q: The Original Sayings of Jesus* (Berkeley: Ulysses Press, 1996), 14-15.

[9] All the following quotes from Q are from Matthew unless otherwise stated.

[10] Meier, *Marginal Jew*, 2:5.

[11] Ibid., 2:101.

[12] Theissen and Merz, *The Historical Jesus*, 187.

[13] Isaac Cogdal to B. F. Irwin, April 10, 1874, as quoted in Walsh, *The Shadows Rise*, 82; Abraham Lincoln, "Speech at Columbus, Ohio," September 16, 1859, in Basler et al., *Collected Works*, 3:410.

[14] Abraham Lincoln to Noah Brooks, December 6, 1864, in Basler et al., *Collected Works*, 8:154-155.

15 Dunn, *Theology of Paul*, 191; Sanders, *Historical Figure of Jesus*, 169.

16 James D. G. Dunn, *Christianity in the Making*, vol. 1: *Jesus Remembered* (Grand Rapids: William B. Eerdmans, 2003), 412-417.

17 Abraham Lincoln, "Fragment on Slavery," April 1, 1854, in Basler et al., *Collected Works*, 2:222-223.

18 Meier, *Marginal Jew*, 2:291-293.

19 John P. Meier, *A Marginal Jew: Rethinking the Historical Jesus*, vol. 3: *Companions and Competitors* (New York: Doubleday, 2001), 2.

20 Richard A. Horsley and Neil Asher Silberman, *The Message and the Kingdom: How Jesus and Paul Ignited a Revolution and Transformed the Ancient World* (New York: Grosset/Putnam, 1997), 53-54.

21 Abraham Lincoln, "Second Inaugural Address," March 4, 1865, in Basler et al., *Collected Works*, 8:333.

22 Doris Kearns Goodwin, *Team of Rivals: The Political Genius of Abraham Lincoln* (New York: Simon & Schuster, 2005), 509.

23 Dunn, *Theology of Paul*, 608.

24 Peter Kirby, "Cornelius Tacitus," *Early Christian Writings.* http://www.earlychristianwritings.com/tacitus.html/ (accessed July 13, 2006); Fredricksen, *Jesus of Nazareth*, 251.

25 Raymond E. Brown, *The Virginal Conception and Bodily Resurrection of Jesus* (New York: Paulist Press, 1973), 108-109.

26 Sanders, *Historical Figure of Jesus*, 278; John P. Meier as quoted in John Bookser Feister, "Finding the Historical Jesus: An Interview with John P. Meier," *St. Anthony Messenger* (December 1997). http://www.americancatholic.org/Messenger/Dec1997/feature3.asp/ (accessed July 13, 2006).

27 Raymond E.Brown, *Introduction to the New Testament* (New York: Doubleday, 1997), 407; Meier, *Marginal Jew*, vol. 1, 45; Günthter Bornkamm, *Paul* (New York: Harper & Row, 1971), 110.

28 See Carol J. Schlueter, *Filling up the Measure: Polemical Hyperbole in 1 Thessalonians 2.14-16* (Sheffield: Sheffield Academic Press, 1994).

[29] Neely, *Abraham Lincoln Encyclopedia*, 164.

[30] Jackson J. Spielvogel, *Western Civilization*, 2 vols. (St. Paul: West Publishing Company, 1991), 1:199.

[31] Horsley and Silberman, *Message and the Kingdom*, 121.

[32] Abraham Lincoln, "Reply to Mayor Alexander Henry at Philadelphia, Pennsylvania," February 12, 1861, in Basler et al., *Collected Works*, 4:239.

[33] Abraham Lincoln as quoted by Isaac Cogdal to B. F. Irwin, April 10, 1874, as quoted in Walsh, *The Shadows Rise*, 81-82.

[34] N. T. Wright, *What Saint Paul Really Said: Was Paul of Tarsus the Real Founder of Christianity?* (Grand Rapids: William B. Eerdmans, 1997), 72; James W. Keys in Wilson and Davis, *Herndon's Informants*, 464.

[35] Marcus Borg, "Jesus and God," in Borg and Wright, *The Meaning of Jesus*, 153.

[36] N. T. Wright, "The Divinity of Jesus," in Borg and Wright, *The Meaning of Jesus*, 162.

[37] Abraham Lincoln, "Speech at Chicago," July 10, 1858, in Basler et al., *Collected Works*, 2:501.

[38] Temple, *From Skeptic to Prophet*, 371; Hurtado, *Lord Jesus Christ*, 563-588.

[39] Herndon and Weik, *Herndon's Life of Lincoln*, 479.

[40] Abraham Lincoln, "Temperance Address," February 22, 1842, in Basler et al., *Collected Works*, 1:276.

[41] Abraham Lincoln to John M. Peck, May 21, 1864, in ibid., 1:473.

[42] Abraham Lincoln as quoted in Fehrenbacher and Fehrenbacher, *Recollected Words*, 106; Abraham Lincoln to George B. Ide, James R. Doolittle, and A. Hubbell, May 30, 1864, in Basler et al., *Collected Works*, 7:368.

[43] Henry V. Jaffa, *A New Birth of Freedom: Abraham Lincoln and the Coming of the Civil War* (Lanham, Md.: Rowman & Littlefield, 2000), 155.

[44] Abraham Lincoln to John D. Johnston, January 12, 1851, in Basler et al., *Collected Works*, 2:97.

[45] Albert A. Woldman, *Lawyer Lincoln* (New York; Carroll & Graf, 1994), 197-198.

[46] Arthur M. Schlesinger, Jr., *The Age of Jackson* (Boston: Little, Brown, 1953), 35.

[47] Abraham Lincoln, "Speech in Chicago, Illinois," July 10, 1858, in Basler et al., *Collected Works*, 2:501.

[48] Abraham Lincoln, "Speech in Springfield, Illinois," July 17, 1858, in ibid., 2:510-511.

[49] Abraham Lincoln, "Reply to a New York Delegation," March 4, 1861, in ibid., 4:272.

[50] Abraham Lincoln, "Fragment on Pro-Slavery Theology," October 1, 1858, in ibid., 3:204.

[51] Dittenhoefer, *How We Elected Lincoln*, 11; Stephen A. Douglas, "Senator Douglas's Reply," Quincy, Illinois, October 13, 1858, in Basler et al., *Collected Works*, 3:275; Abraham Lincoln, "Notes for Speeches at Columbus and Cincinnati, Ohio," September 16, 17, 1859, in ibid., 3:426.

[52] Abraham Lincoln to George B. Ide, James R. Doolittle, and A. Hubbell, May 30, 1864, in ibid., 7:368; Abraham Lincoln, "Second Inaugural," March 4, 1865, in ibid., 8:333; Abraham Lincoln as quoted in Fehrenbacher and Fehrenbacher, *Recollected Words*, 435.

[53] Abraham Lincoln, "Speech at Cincinnati, Ohio," September 17, 1859, in Basler et al., *Collected Works*, 3:462.

[54] Abraham Lincoln to George D. Prentice, October 29, 1860 in ibid., 4:135.

[55] Abraham Lincoln as quoted in Fehrenbacher and Fehrenbacher, *Recollected Words*, 297.

[56] Trueblood, *Theologian of American Anguish*, 52.

57 Abraham Lincoln to George B. Ide, James R. Doolittle, and A. Hubbell, May 30, 1864, in Basler et al., *Collected Works*, 7:368.

58 Abraham Lincoln, "Second Inaugural," March 4, 1865, in ibid., 8:333.

59 "Popular American Hymns of the Eighteenth and Nineteenth Centuries," *PD Music Site Index.* http://www.pdmusic.org/hymns.html/ (accessed July 8, 2007).

Chapter 5: War and Death

1 This reversal of fortune is told in most general Civil War histories. The best short account is James M. McPherson, *The Battle Cry of Freedom: The Civil War Era* (New York: Ballantine Books, 1988), 490-524.

2 Lincoln related that he made this promise to his cabinet see David Herbert Donald, ed., *Inside Lincoln's Cabinet: The Civil War Diaries of Salmon P. Chase* (New York: Longmans, Green, 1954), 149-150.

3 Abraham Lincoln, "Address to the New Jersey Senate at Trenton, New Jersey," February 21, 1861, in Basler et al., *Collected Works*, 4:236.

4 Ronald C. White, Jr., *The Eloquent President: A Portrait of Lincoln Through His Words* (New York: Random House, 2005), 54.

5 Abraham Lincoln, "First Inaugural Address—Final Text," March 4, 1861, in Basler et al., *Collected Works*, 4:271.

6 Abraham Lincoln as quoted in Temple, *From Skeptic to Prophet*, 141; Temple, 140, 142, 143,144.

7 Abraham Lincoln, April 24, 1861, as quoted in Tyler Dennett, ed., *Lincoln and the Civil War: In the Diaries and Letters of John Hay* (New York: Da Capo Press, 1988), 11.

8 William Lee Miller, *Lincoln's Virtues: An Ethical Biography* (New York: Knopf, 2002), 56.

9 A. K. McClure in Emmanuel Hertz, ed., *Lincoln Talks: An Oral Biography* (New York: Bramhall House, 1986), 375-376. McClure tells a somewhat different version of the story in Alexander McClure, *Abraham Lincoln and Men of War-Times: Some Personal Recollections of War and*

Politics During the Lincoln Administration (Philadelphia: Times Publishing, 1892), 67-69.

[10] Burlingame, *Inner World of Abraham Lincoln*, 79; Henry Whitney as quoted in ibid., 79; John Hay as quoted in ibid., 80.

[11] Margaret Leech, *Reveille in Washington: 1860-1865* (New York: Harper & Brothers, 1941), 81.

[12] Burlingame, *Inner World of Abraham Lincoln*, 80; Abraham Lincoln to Ephraim D. and Phoebe Ellsworth, May 25, 1861, in Basler et al., *Collected Works*, 4:386.

[13] Beveridge, *Abraham Lincoln*, 1:389.

[14] Herndon and Weik, *Herndon's Life of Lincoln*, 158; Riddle, *Lincoln Runs for Congress*, 161.

[15] McPherson, *Battle Cry of Freedom*, 362; Charles Carlton Coffin, "Lincoln's First Nomination and His Visit to Richmond," in Rice, *Reminiscences of Abraham Lincoln*, 176-177.

[16] Ruth Painter Randall, *Lincoln's Sons* (Boston: Little, Brown, 1955), 93.

[17] Burlingame, *Inner World of Abraham Lincoln*, 65, 66; Willie Lincoln in Harold Holzer, ed., *Lincoln as I Knew Him: Gossip, Tributes & Revelations from His Best Friends and Worst Enemies* (Chapel Hill: Algonquin Books, 1999), 28.

[18] William Herndon to Jesse Weik, February 18, 1887, in Hertz, *Hidden Lincoln*, 176-177.

[19] Burlingame, *Inner World of Abraham Lincoln*, 66; Temple, *From Skeptic to Prophet*, 182.

[20] Randall, *Lincoln's Sons*, 99, 100.

[21] John Nicolay, February 20, 1862, in Michael Burlingame, ed., *With Lincoln in the White House: Letters, Memoranda, and Other Writings of John G. Nicolay, 1860-1865* (Carbondale: Southern Illinois University Press, 2000), 71; Abraham Lincoln in Fehrenbacher and Fehrenbacher, *Recollected Words*, 78; Abraham Lincoln as quoted in W. Emerson Reck,

A. *Lincoln: His Last 24 Hours* (Columbia: University of South Carolina Press, 1987), 47.

[22] Elizabeth Keckley, *Behind the Scenes or Thirty Years a Slave, and Four Years in the White House* (Oxford: Oxford University Press, 1988), 102-104.

[23] Donald, *Lincoln*, 336.

[24] Noah Brooks as quote in Barton, *Soul of Abraham Lincoln*, 327; Mary Todd Lincoln in Wilson and Davis, *Herndon's Informants*, 360; Donald, *Lincoln*, 337; Mary Todd Lincoln to James Smith, June 8, 1870, in Turner and Turner, *Mary Todd Lincoln*, 567-568.

[25] Randall, *Lincoln's Sons*, 101; Phineas Gurley as quoted in Temple, *From Skeptic to Prophet*, 187.

[26] Ibid., 188.

[27] Ibid., 189; Jones, *Lincoln and the Preachers*, 37, 41.

[28] Phineas Gurley as quoted in Jones, *Lincoln and the Preachers*, 37; Temple, *From Skeptic to Prophet*, 144.

[29] Barton, *Soul of Abraham Lincoln*, 87; Phineas Gurley as quoted in ibid., 326.

[30] Neely, *Abraham Lincoln Encyclopedia*, 277-278; Matthew Simpson, "Under the Permissive Hand of God," May 4, 1865, in Waldo W. Braden, ed., *Building the Myth: Selected Speeches Memorializing Abraham Lincoln* (Urbana: University of Illinois Press, 1990), 82, 83.

[31] For Lincoln's original emancipation scheme see James G. Randall, *Lincoln the President: Springfield to Gettysburg*, 2 vols. (New York: Dodd, Mead, 1945), 2:126-150; Abraham Lincoln to Horace Greeley, August 22, 1862, in Basler et al., *Collected Works*, 5:389.

[32] Abraham Lincoln to Albert G. Hodges, April 4, 1864, in Basler et al., *Collected Works*, 7:281; Abraham Lincoln, "Reply to Emancipation Memorial Presented by Chicago Christians of All Denominations," September 13, 1862, in ibid., 5:419-420, 423.

[33] Allen C. Guelzo, *Lincoln's Emancipation Proclamation: The End of Slavery in America* (New York: Simon & Schuster, 2004), 123.

[34] Ibid., 151-152.

[35] Salmon P. Chase in Donald, *Inside Lincoln's Cabinet*, 149; Artemus Ward, "High-Handed Outrage at Utica," as quoted in Barton, *Soul of Abraham Lincoln*, 308.

[36] Salmon P. Chase in Donald, *Inside Lincoln's Cabinet*, 149-150; Carpenter, *Inner Life of Abraham Lincoln*, 89-90.

[37] Gideon Welles, September 22, 1862, in John T. Morse, Jr., ed., *Diary of Gideon Welles: Secretary of the Navy Under Lincoln and Johnson*, 3 vols. (Boston: Houghton Mifflin, 1911), 1:142-143; Gideon Welles as quoted in Goodwin, *Team of Rivals*, 482.

[38] Guelzo, *Lincoln's Emancipation Proclamation*, 153; Abraham Lincoln, "Response to Serenade in Honor of Emancipation Proclamation," September 24, 1862, in Basler et al., *Collected Works*, 5:438.

[39] Abraham Lincoln as quoted by Lot M. Morrill in Burlingame, *Oral History of Abraham Lincoln*, 54-55; Orville Browning, June 17, 1865, in ibid., 5.

[40] Matthew Simpson as quoted in Temple, *From Skeptic to Prophet*, 353; Abraham Lincoln in Fehrenbacher and Fehrenbacher, *Recollected Words*,

[41] Abraham Lincoln to Eliza P. Guerney, October 26, 1862, in Leidner, *Lincoln on God and Country*, 106; Abraham Lincoln to Eliza P. Guerney, September 1864, in ibid., 110.

[42] Gideon A. Welles, September 2, 1862, in Morse, ed., *Diary of Gideon Welles*, 1:105; Abraham Lincoln, "Meditation on the Divine Will," September 2, 1862, in Basler et al., *Collected Works*, 5:403-404. Douglas Wilson has discovered that this note was probably written in 1864. See Douglas L. Wilson, *Lincoln's Sword: The Presidency and the Power of Words* (New York: Knopf, 2006), 254-256; John Hay as quoted in Trueblood, *Theologian of American Anguish*, 40.

[43] Abraham Lincoln to Albert G. Hodges, April 4, 1864, in Basler et al., *Collected Works*, 7:282.

[44] Glen E. Thurow, "Abraham Lincoln's Political Religion," in Gabor S. Boritt, ed., *The Historian's Lincoln: Pseudohistory, Psychohistory, and History* (Urbana: University of Illinois Press, 1996), 129.

[45] H. L. Mencken as quoted in Neely, *Abraham Lincoln Encyclopedia*, 207.

[46] Abraham Lincoln, "Proclamation of a National Fast Day," in Basler et al., *Collected Works*, 4:482.

[47] Joseph R. Fornieri, *Abraham Lincoln's Political Faith* (DeKalb: Northern Illinois University Press, 2003), 36.

[48] Abraham Lincoln, "Proclamation of Thanksgiving for Victories," April 10, 1862, in Basler et al., *Collected Works*, 5:185-186.

[49] Abraham Lincoln to Arnold Fischel, December 14, 1861, in Basler et al., *Collected Works*, 5:69; Henry Halleck as quoted in Mark E. Neely, Jr., *The Last Best Hope: Abraham Lincoln and the Promise of America* (Cambridge, Mass.: Harvard University Press, 1993), 149.

[50] Abraham Lincoln to Edwin M. Stanton, February 5, 1864, in Basler et al., *Collected Works*, 7:169.

[51] John Nicolay to William Herndon, May 27, 1865, as quoted in Herndon and Weik, *Herndon's Life of Lincoln*, 357.

[52] Joshua F. Speed in Wilson and Davis, *Herndon's Informants*, 31; Joshua F. Speed to William Herndon, January 12, 1866, in ibid., 157.

[53] Donald, *"We Are Lincoln Men,"* 64. Donald makes some tenuous claims to back up his assertion on this point including the idea that since Denis Hanks's decades-later account of Lincoln's mother's death is silent on whether she will see them in heaven is evidence that she never believed in the afterlife.

[54] Joshua F. Speed to William Herndon, January 12, 1866, in Wilson and Davis, *Herndon's Informants*, 156.

55 James A. Rawley, "Introduction," in Isaac N. Arnold, *The Life of Abraham Lincoln* (Lincoln: University of Nebraska Press, 1994), xiv-xv; Mark E. Neely, Jr., and R. Gerald McMurtry, *The Insanity File: The Case of Mary Todd Lincoln* (Carbondale: Southern Illinois University Press, 1986), 17; Arnold, *The Life of Abraham Lincoln*, 446-447.

56 F. B. Carpenter and Mary Todd Lincoln, as quoted in Burkhimer, *100 Essential Lincoln Books*, 3-4; Carpenter, *Inner Life of Abraham Lincoln*, 185-186, 186.

57 Herbert Mitgang, "Introduction," in Noah Brooks, *Washington in Lincoln's Time* (New York: Rinehart, 1958), 6-11; Neely, *Abraham Lincoln Encyclopedia*, 38.

58 Noah Brooks, "How the President Looks," December 4, 1862, in Michael Burlingame, ed., *Lincoln Observed: Civil War Dispatches of Noah Brooks* (Baltimore: John Hopkins University Press, 1998), 13.

59 Noah Brooks, "The New Term," November 11, 1864, in ibid., 145.

60 Temple, *From Skeptic to Prophet*, 313; Brooks, *Washington in Lincoln's Time*, 61.

61 Noah Brooks to Isaac P. Langworthy, May 10, 1865, in Burlingame, *Lincoln Observed*, 195-196; Noah Brooks to James A. Reed, December 31, 1872, as quoted in Barton, *Soul of Abraham Lincoln*, 327.

62 Abraham Lincoln as quoted in Burlingame, *Lincoln Observed*, 210; Noah Brooks, "Personal Recollections of Abraham Lincoln," in ibid., 211.

63 Michael Burlingame, "Editor's Introduction," in William O. Stoddard, *Inside the White House in War Times: Memoirs and Reports of Lincoln's Secretary* (Lincoln: University of Nebraska Press, 2000), x-xv, xx-xxi.

64 Stoddard, *Inside the White House in War Times*, 176.

65 William O. Stoddard to Francis E. Abbot, February 18, 1870, as quoted in ibid., 215-216.

66 David Homer Bates, *Lincoln in the Telegraph Office: Recollections of the United States Military Telegraph Corps During the Civil War* (Lincoln: University of Nebraska Press, 1995), 215-216.

67 Orville H. Browning to Isaac Arnold, 1872, in Burlingame, *Oral History of Abraham Lincoln*, 131.

68 Temple, *From Skeptic to Prophet*, 370.

69 Edward O. Steers, Jr., "Was Mistah Abe Babsized?" *Lincoln Herald* 101, no. 4 (Winter 1999), 164-165; Guelzo, *Redeemer President*, 446.

70 Benjamin Quarles, *Lincoln and the Negro* (Oxford: Oxford University Press, 1991), 207-208.

71 Wolf, *Almost Chosen People*, 132-133.

72 Ibid., 133-134.

73 Dittenhoefer, *How We Elected Lincoln*, 12.

Chapter 6: The Second Inauguration

1 Donald, *Lincoln*, 565; Hans L. Trefousse, *Andrew Johnson: A Biography* (New York: W. W. Norton, 1989), 189-191.

2 Guelzo, *Redeemer President*, 416.

3 Ronald C. White, Jr., *Lincoln's Greatest Speech: The Second Inaugural* (New York: Simon & Schuster, 2002), 39; William C. Davis, *Lincoln's Men: How President Lincoln Became a Father to an Army and a Nation* (New York: Free Press, 1999), 223.

4 White, *Lincoln's Greatest Speech*, 41-42; Abraham Lincoln, "Mr. Lincoln's Reply," August 21, 1858, in Basler et al., *Collected Works*, 3:14; Brooks, *Washington in Lincoln's Time*, 213.

5 Fornieri, *Abraham Lincoln's Political Faith*, 165; Abraham Lincoln, "Second Inaugural Address," March 4, 1865, in Basler et al., *Collected Works*, 8:332.

6 White, *Lincoln's Greatest Speech*, 48.

7 Lincoln, "Second Inaugural Address," March 4, 1865, in Basler et al., *Collected Works*, 8:332; Mark A. Noll, "'Both . . . Pray to the Same God': The Singularity of Lincoln's Faith in the Era of the Civil War," *Journal of the Abraham Lincoln Association* 18, no. 1 (Winter 1997), 7; Guelzo, *Redeemer President*, 418.

8 Lincoln, "Second Inaugural Address," March 4, 1865, in Basler et al., *Collected Works*, 8:332-333.

9 Earl Schwartz, "'A Poor Hand to Quote Scripture': Lincoln and Genesis 3:19," *Journal of the Abraham Lincoln Association* 22, no. 2 (Summer 2002), 39; Abraham Lincoln, "Address Before the Wisconsin State Agricultural Society, Milwaukee, Wisconsin," September 30, 1859, in Basler et al., *Collected Works*, 3:478.

10 Noll, "Both . . . Pray to the Same God," 13; Strozier, *Lincoln's Quest for Union*, 64-65.

11 Lincoln, "Second Inaugural Address," March 4, 1865, in Basler et al., *Collected Works*, 8:333.

12 Guelzo, *Redeemer President*, 420; Abraham Lincoln as quoted in Thomas, *Abraham Lincoln*, 512.

13 Temple, *From Skeptic to Prophet*, 285-286.

14 *New York World* as quoted in William C. Harris, *Lincoln's Last Months* (Cambridge, Mass.: Belknap Press of Harvard University Press, 2004), 149; *Detroit Free Press* as quoted in ibid.

15 Noll, "'Both . . . Pray to the Same God,'" 2-3.

16 *The Spectator* as quoted in James G. Randall and Richard N. Current, *Lincoln the President: Last Full Measure* (New York: Dodd, Mead, 1955), 343; Duke of Argyll as quoted in ibid.

17 Lord Charnwood, *Abraham Lincoln* (Garden City, N.Y.: Garden City, 1917), 441.

18 Abraham Lincoln to Thurlow Weed, March 15, 1865, in Basler et al., *Collected Works*, 8:356.

19 White, *Lincoln's Greatest Speech*, 185; John Wilkes Booth, "To Whom it May Concern," November 1864, in Asia Clarke Booth, *John Wilkes Booth: A Sister's Memoir* (Jackson: University of Mississippi Press, 1996), 107, 110.

Conclusion

[1] Quarles, *Lincoln and the Negro*, 239-249.

[2] Edward O. Steers, Jr., *Blood on the Moon: The Assassination of Abraham Lincoln* (Lexington: University of Kentucky Press, 2001), 273.

[3] Mary Todd Lincoln, September 1866, in Wilson and Davis, *Herndon's Informants*, 360; Robert G. Ingersoll, "The Religious Belief of Abraham Lincoln," May 28, 1896, in C. P. Farrell, ed., *The Complete Works of Robert G. Ingersoll*, 12 vols. (New York: Dresden, 1900), 12:254.

[4] William Herndon as quoted in Richard N. Current, *The Lincoln Nobody Knows* (New York: Hill and Wang, 1995), 65; Herndon and Weik, *Herndon's Life of Lincoln*, 355.

[5] Abraham Lincoln as quoted in Trueblood, *Theologian of American Anguish*, 110.

BIBLIOGRAPHY

Allison, Dale C. *Jesus of Nazareth: Millenarian Prophet.* Minneapolis: Fortress Press, 1998.

Angle, Paul M. *Here I Have Lived: A History of Lincoln's Springfield.* Springfield, Ill.: Abraham Lincoln Association, 1935.

Arnold, Isaac N. *The Life of Abraham Lincoln.* Lincoln: University of Nebraska Press, 1994.

Baker, Jean H. *Mary Todd Lincoln: A Biography.* New York: W. W. Norton, 1987.

Baringer, William. *Lincoln's Rise to Power.* Boston: Little, Brown, 1937.

_____. *A House Dividing: Lincoln as President-Elect.* Springfield, Ill.: Abraham Lincoln Association, 1945.

Barton, William E. *The Soul of Abraham Lincoln.* New York: George H. Doran, 1920.

_____. *The Life of Abraham Lincoln.* 2 vols. Indianapolis: Bobbs-Merrill, 1925.

_____. *The Lineage of Lincoln.* Indianapolis: Bobbs-Merrill, 1929.

Basler, Roy P., Marion Dolores Pratt, and Lloyd A. Dunlap, eds. *The Collected Works of Abraham Lincoln.* 8 vols. and index. New Brunswick, N.J.: Rutgers University Press, 1953.

Bates, David Homer. *Lincoln in the Telegraph Office: Recollections of the United States Military Telegraph Corps During the Civil War.* Lincoln: University of Nebraska Press, 1995.

Beveridge, Albert J. *Abraham Lincoln: 1809-1858.* 2 vols. Boston: Houghton Mifflin, 1928.

Booth, Asia Clarke. *John Wilkes Booth: A Sister's Memoir,* ed. Terry Alfred. Jackson: University of Mississippi Press, 1996.

Borg, Marcus. *The Lost Gospel Q: The Original Sayings of Jesus.* Berkeley: Ulysses Press, 1996.

———. "Jesus and God." In Marcus J. Borg and N. T. Wright, *The Meaning of Jesus: Two Visions,* 145-156. San Francisco: HarperCollins, 1999.

———. "The Meaning of the Birth Stories." In Marcus J. Borg and N. T. Wright,*The Meaning of Jesus: Two Visions,* 179-186. San Francisco: HarperCollins, 1999.

Borg, Marcus J., and N. T. Wright. *The Meaning of Jesus: Two Visions.* San Francisco: HarperCollins, 1999.

Boritt, Gabor S., ed. *The Historian's Lincoln: Pseudohistory, Psychohistory, and History.* Urbana: University of Illinois Press, 1996.

———. *The Lincoln Enigma: The Changing Face of an American Icon.* Oxford: Oxford University Press, 2001.

Bornkamm, Günther. *Paul.* 1969. Translated by D. M. G. Stalker. New York: Harper & Row, 1971.

Braden, Waldo W., ed. *Building the Myth: Selected Speeches Memorializing Abraham Lincoln.* Urbana: University of Illinois Press, 1990.

Brodie, Fawn M. *Thomas Jefferson: An Intimate History.* New York: W. W. Norton, 1974.

Brooks, Noah. *Washington in Lincoln's Time.* New York: Rinehart, 1958.

Brown, Raymond E. *The Virginal Conception and Bodily Resurrection of Jesus*. New York: Paulist Press, 1973.

———. *An Introduction to the New Testament*. New York: Doubleday, 1997.

Bruce, Robert V. "The Riddle of Death." In *The Lincoln Enigma: The Changing Face of an American Icon*, ed. Gabor S. Boritt, 130-145. Oxford: Oxford University Press, 2001.

Burkhimer, Michael. *100 Essential Lincoln Books*. Nashville: Cumberland House, 2003.

Burlingame, Michael. *The Inner World of Abraham Lincoln*. Urbana: University of Illinois Press, 1994.

———, ed. *An Oral History of Abraham Lincoln: John G. Nicolay's Interviews and Essays*. Carbondale: Southern Illinois University Press, 1996.

———. *Lincoln Observed: Civil War Dispatches of Noah Brooks*. Baltimore: John Hopkins University Press, 1998.

———. *At Lincoln's Side: John Hay's Civil War Correspondence and Selected Writings*. Carbondale: Southern Illinois University Press, 2000.

———. *With Lincoln in the White House: Letters, Memoranda, and Other Writings of John G. Nicolay, 1860-1865*. Carbondale: Southern Illinois University Press, 2000.

Burns, Robert. *Robert Burns: Selected Poems*. New York: Penguin Books, 1993.

Carpenter, Francis B. *The Inner Life of Abraham Lincoln: Six Months in the White House*. Lincoln: University of Nebraska Press, 1995.

Carwardine, Richard J. "Lincoln, Evangelical Religion, and American Political Culture in the Era of the Civil War." *Journal of the Abraham Lincoln Association* 18, no. 1 (Winter 1997): 27-56.

———. *Lincoln: A Life of Purpose and Power*. New York: Knopf, 2006.

Charnwood, Lord. *Abraham Lincoln*. Garden City, N.Y.: Garden City
    Publishing Company, 1917.

Chesterton, G. K. *What's Wrong with the World?* San Francisco: Ignatius
    Press, 1994.

Coffin, Charles Carlton. "Lincoln's First Nomination and His Visit to
    Richmond." In *Reminiscences of Abraham Lincoln by Distinguished
    Men of his Time*, ed. Allen Thorndike Rice, 165-188. New York:
    Harper and Brothers, 1909.

Current, Richard N. *The Lincoln Nobody Knows*. New York: Hill and
    Wang, 1995.

Davis, William C. *Lincoln's Men: How President Lincoln Became a
    Father to an Army and a Nation*. New York: The Free Press, 1999.

Dennett, Tyler, ed. *Lincoln and the Civil War: In the Diaries and Letters
    of John Hay*. New York: Da Capo Press, 1988.

Dittenhoefer, Abram J. *How We Elected Lincoln: Personal Recollections*.
    Philadelphia: University of Pennsylvania Press, 2005.

Donald, David Herbert. *Lincoln's Herndon: A Biography*. New York: Da
    Capo Press, 1989.

Donald, David Herbert, ed. *Inside Lincoln's Cabinet: The Civil War
    Diaries of Salmon P. Chase*. New York: Longmans, Green, 1954.

_____. *Lincoln Reconsidered: Essays on the Civil War Era*. New York:
    Vintage Books, 1989.

_____. *Lincoln*. New York: Simon & Schuster, 1995.

_____. *"We Are Lincoln Men": Abraham Lincoln and His Friends*.
    New York: Simon & Schuster, 2003.

Dunn, James D. G. *The Theology of Paul the Apostle*. Grand Rapids:
    William B. Eerdmans, 1998.

_____. *Christianity in the Making*, Vol. 1: *Jesus Remembered*. Grand
    Rapids: William B. Eerdmans, 2003.

Emesron, Jason. "'Of Such Is the Kingdom of Heaven': The Mystery of

'Little Eddie.'" *Journal of the Illinois State Historical Society* (Autumn 1999). http://www.findarticles.com/p/articles/mi_qa3945/is_199910/ai_n88 62405/ (accessed July 13, 2006).

Farrell, C. P., ed. *The Complete Works of Robert G. Ingersoll.* 12 vols. New York: Dresden, 1900.

Fehrenbacher, Don E., and Virginia Fehrenbacher, eds. *Recollected Words of Abraham Lincoln.* Stanford: Stanford University Press, 1996.

Feister, John B. "Finding the Historical Jesus: An Interview with John P. Meier." *St. Anthony Messenger* (December 1997). http://www.americancatholic.org/Messenger/Dec1997/feature3.asp/ (accessed July 13, 2006).

Fleischner, Jennifer. *Mrs. Lincoln and Mrs. Keckly: The Remarkable Story of the Friendship Between a First Lady and a Former Slave.* New York: Broadway Books, 2003.

Foner, Eric. *Free Soil, Free Labor, Free Men: The Ideology of the Republican Party Before the Civil War.* New York: Oxford University Press, 1970.

Fornieri, Joseph R. *Abraham Lincoln's Political Faith.* DeKalb: Northern Illinois University Press, 2003.

Frank, John P. *Lincoln as a Lawyer.* Chicago: Americana House, 1991.

Fredricksen, Paula. *Jesus of Nazareth: King of the Jews.* New York: Vintage Books, 1999.

Funk, Robert W. and The Jesus Seminar. *The Acts of Jesus: What Did Jesus Really Do?* San Francisco: HarperSanFrancisco, 1998.

Goff, John S. *Robert Todd Lincoln: A Man in His Own Right.* Norman: University of Oklahoma Press, 1969.

Goodwin, Doris Kearns. *Team of Rivals: The Political Genius of Abraham Lincoln.* New York: Simon & Schuster, 2005.

Guelzo, Allen C. "Abraham Lincoln and the Doctrine of Necessity." *Journal of the Abraham Lincoln Association* 18, no. 1 (Winter 1997): 57-82.

———. *Abraham Lincoln: Redeemer President*. Grand Rapids: William B. Eerdmans, 1999.

———. "Holland's Informants: The Construction of Josiah Holland's 'Life of Abraham Lincoln.'" *Journal of the Abraham Lincoln Association* 23, no. 1 (Winter 2002): 1-54.

———. *Lincoln's Emancipation Proclamation: The End of Slavery in America*. New York: Simon & Schuster, 2004.

Harper, Robert S. *Lincoln and the Press*. New York: McGraw-Hill, 1951.

Harris, William C. *Lincoln's Last Months*. Cambridge, Mass.: Belknap Press of Harvard University Press, 2004.

Havlick, Robert J. "Abraham Lincoln and the Reverend Dr. James Smith: Lincoln's Presbyterian Experience of Springfield." *Journal of the Illinois Historical Society* (Autumn 1999). http://www.findarticles.com/p/articles/mi_qa3945/is_199910/ai_n8861124/ (accessed July 13, 2006).

———. "Some Influences of Thomas Paine's 'Age of Reason' Upon Abraham Lincoln." *Lincoln Herald* 104, no. 2 (Summer 2002): 61-71.

Herndon, William H., and Jesse W. Weik. *Herndon's Life of Lincoln*. New York: Da Capo Press, 1983.

Hertz, Emmanuel, ed. *The Hidden Lincoln: From the Letters and Papers of William H. Herndon*. Garden City, N.Y.: Blue Ribbon Books, 1938.

———. *Lincoln Talks: An Oral Biography*. New York: Bramhall House, 1986.

Holland, Josiah G. *The Life of Abraham Lincoln*. Springfield, Ill.: Samuel Bowles, 1866.

Holzer, Harold, ed. *Lincoln as I Knew Him: Gossip, Tributes and Revelations from His Best Friends and Worst Enemies.* Chapel Hill: Algonquin Books, 1999.

Horsley, Richard A., and Neil Asher Silberman. *The Message and the Kingdom: How Jesus and Paul Ignited a Revolution and Transformed the Ancient World.* New York: Grosset/Putnam, 1997.

Howe, Daniel Walker. *The Political Culture of American Whigs.* Chicago: University of Chicago Press, 1979.

Hurtado, Larry W. *Lord Jesus Christ: Devotion to Jesus in Earliest Christianity.* Grand Rapids: William B. Eerdmans, 2003.

Ingersoll, Robert G. "The Gentlest Memory of Our World." In *Reminiscences of Abraham Lincoln by Distinguished Men of His Time*, ed. Allen Thorndike Rice, 421-428. New York: Harper and Brothers, 1909.

Jaffa, Henry V. *A New Birth of Freedom: Abraham Lincoln and the Coming of the Civil War.* Lanham, Md.: Rowman & Littlefield, 2000.

Jones, Edgar DeWitt. *Lincoln and the Preachers.* Freeport: Harper & Brothers, 1948.

Keckley, Elizabeth. *Behind the Scenes or Thirty Years a Slave, and Four Years in the White House.* Oxford: Oxford University Press, 1988.

Kirby, Peter. "Cornelius Tacitus," *Early Christian Writings.* http://www.earlychristianwritings.com/tacitus.html/ (accessed July 13, 2006).

———. *Early Christian Writings.* http://www.earlychristianwritings.com/ (accessed July 13, 2006).

Kloppenberg, John S. *The Formation of Q: Trajectories in Ancient Wisdom Collections.* New York: Trinity Press International, 2000.

Lamon, Ward Hill. *The Life of Abraham Lincoln: From His Birth to His Inauguration as President.* Lincoln: University of Nebraska Press, 1999.

_____. *Recollections of Abraham Lincoln: 1847-1865*. Lincoln: University of Nebraska Press, 1995.

Leech, Margaret. *Reveille in Washington: 1860-1865*. New York: Harper & Brothers, 1941.

Leidner, Gordon. *Lincoln on God and Country*. Shippensburg, Pa.: White Mane Publishing, 2000.

Luthin, Reinhard H. *The Real Abraham Lincoln: A Complete One Volume History of His Life and Times*. Englewood Cliffs, N.J.: Prentice-Hall, 1960.

Mack, Burton L. The *Lost Gospel: The Book of Q and Christian Origins*. San Francisco: HarperSanFrancisco, 1993.

Malone, Dumas, and Basil Rauch. *Empire for Liberty: The Genesis and Growth of the United States of America*. 2 vols. New York: Appleton-Century-Crofts, 1960.

McClure, Alexander. *Abraham Lincoln and Men of War-Times: Some Personal Recollections of War and Politics During the Lincoln Administration*. Philadelphia: Times Publishing, 1892.

McPherson, James M. *The Battle Cry of Freedom: The Civil War Era*. New York: Ballantine Books, 1988.

Meier, John P. *A Marginal Jew: Rethinking the Historical Jesus*, Vol. 1: *The Roots of the Problem and the Person*. New York: Doubleday, 1991.

_____. *A Marginal Jew: Rethinking the Historical Jesus*, Vol. 2: *Mentor, Message, and Miracles*. New York: Doubleday, 1994.

_____. *A Marginal Jew: Rethinking the Historical Jesus*, Vol. 3: *Companions and Competitors*. New York: Doubleday, 2001.

Miers, Earl Schenk, ed. *Lincoln Day by Day: A Chronology, 1809-1865*. 3 vols. in 1. Dayton: Morningside, 1991.

Miller, Richard Lawrence. "Lincoln's Suicide Poem: Has it Been Found?" *For the People*. 6, no. 1 (Spring 2004): 1, 6.

Miller, Robert J. "Does Jesus Fulfill Prophecy? Probing Matthew's Gospel." *The Fourth R: An Advocate of Religious Liberty* 16, no. 2 (March-April 2003): 2-8.

Miller, William Lee. *Lincoln's Virtues: An Ethical Biography*. New York: Knopf, 2002.

Morel, Lucas E. *Lincoln's Sacred Effort: Defining Religion's Role in American Self-Government*. Lanham, Md.: Lexington Books, 2000.

Morse, John T., Jr. *Abraham Lincoln*. 2 vols. Boston: Houghton-Mifflin, 1893.

_____, ed. *Diary of Gideon Welles: Secretary of the Navy Under Lincoln and Johnson*. 3 vols. Boston: Houghton Mifflin, 1911.

Morgan, Edmund S. *The Puritan Dilemma: The Story of John Winthrop*. New York: HarperCollins, 1958.

Nagel, Paul C. *Descent from Glory: Four Generations of the John Adams Family*. New York: Oxford University Press, 1983.

Neely, Mark E., Jr. *The Abraham Lincoln Encyclopedia*. New York: Da Capo Press, 1982.

_____. *The Last Best Hope: Abraham Lincoln and the Promise of America*. Cambridge, Mass.: Harvard University Press, 1993.

Neely, Mark E., Jr., and R. Gerald McMurtry. *The Insanity File: The Case of Mary Todd Lincoln*. Carbondale: Southern Illinois University Press, 1986.

Noll, Mark A. "'Both…Pray to the Same God': The Singularity of Lincoln's Faith in the Era of the Civil War." *Journal of the Abraham Lincoln Association* 18, no. 1 (Winter 1997): 1-26.

Norton, Roger. *Abraham Lincoln Research Site*. http://members.aol.com/RVSNorton/Lincoln2.html/ (accessed April 20, 2007).

_____. "Eddie Lincoln," *Abraham Lincoln Research Site*. http://home.att.net/~rjnorton/Lincoln67.html/ (accessed April 20, 2007).

Nye, Russel Blaine. *The Cultural Life of the New Nation: 1776-1830.* New York: Harper & Row, 1963.

Oates, Stephen B. *Abraham Lincoln: The Man Behind the Myths.* New York: HarperPerennial, 1984.

Ostendorf, Lloyd. *Lincoln's Photographs: A Complete Album.* Dayton: Rockywood Press, 1998.

Peterson, Merrill D. *Lincoln in American Memory.* Oxford: Oxford University Press, 1994.

Pinkser, Matthew. *Lincoln's Sanctuary: Abraham Lincoln and the Soldier's Home.* Oxford: Oxford University Press, 2003.

"Popular American Hymns of the 18th and 19th Centuries," *PD Music Site Index.* http://www.pdmusic.org/hymns.html/(accessed July 8, 2007).

Quarles, Benjamin. *Lincoln and the Negro.* Oxford: Oxford University Press, 1991.

Randall, James G. *Lincoln the President: Springfield to Gettysburg.* 2 vols. New York: Dodd, Mead, 1945.

Randall, James G., and Richard N. Current. *Lincoln the President: Last Full Measure.* New York: Dodd, Mead, 1955.

Randall, Ruth Painter. *Mary Lincoln: Biography of a Marriage.* Boston: Little, Brown, 1953.

———. *Lincoln's Sons.* Boston: Little, Brown, 1955.

Rankin, Henry B. *Personal Recollections of Abraham Lincoln.* New York: G. P. Putnam's Sons, 1916.

Reck, W. Emerson. *A. Lincoln: His Last Twenty-Four Hours.* Columbia: University of South Carolina Press, 1987.

Reep, Thomas P. *Lincoln at New Salem.* Petersburg, Va.: Old Salem Lincoln League, 1927.

Rice, Allen Thorndike, ed. *Reminiscences of Abraham Lincoln by Distinguished Men of His Time.* New York: Harper and Brothers, 1909.

Riddle, Donald W. *Lincoln Runs for Congress*. New Brunswick, N.J.: Rutgers University Press, 1948.

Sanders, E. P. *The Historical Figure of Jesus*. London: Penguin Books, 1993.

Schlesinger, Jr., Arthur M. *The Age of Jackson*. Boston: Little, Brown, 1953.

Schlueter, Carol J. *Filling up the Measure: Polemical Hyperbole in 1 Thessalonians 2.14-16*. Sheffield: Sheffield Academic Press, 1994.

Schwartz, Earl. "'A Poor Hand to Quote Scripture': Lincoln and Genesis 3:19." *Journal of the Abraham Lincoln Association* 22, no. 2 (Summer 2002): 37-49.

Searcher, Victor. *Lincoln's Journey to Greatness: A Factual Account of the Twelve-Day Inaugural Trip*. Philadelphia: John C. Winston, 1960.

Shenk, Joshua Wolf. *Lincoln's Melancholy: How Depression Challenged a President and Fueled His Greatness*. Boston: Houghton Mifflin, 2005.

Simon, Paul. *Lincoln's Preparation for Greatness: The Illinois Legislature Years*. Urbana: University of Illinois Press, 1971.

Simpson, Matthew. "Under the Permissive Hand of God." In *Building the Myth: Selected Speeches Memorializing Abraham Lincoln*, ed. Waldo W. Braden, 75-86. Urbana: University of Chicago Press, 1990.

Smith, James. *The Christian's Defence, Containing a Fair Statement, and Impartial Examination of the Leading Objections Urged by Infidels Against the Antiquity, Genuineness, Credibility and Inspiration of the Holy Scriptures*, 2 vols. in 1. Cincinnati: J. A. James, 1843.

_____. *A Discourse on the Bottle—Its Evils, and the Remedy: A Vindication of the Liquor-Seller, and the Liquor Drinker, from Certain Aspirations Cast upon Them by Many*. Springfield, Ill.: privately printed, 1853, 1892.

Speed, Joshua F. *Reminiscences of Abraham Lincoln and Notes of a Visit to California: Two Lectures.* Louisville: John P. Morton, 1884.

Spielvogel, Jackson J. *Western Civilization*, 2 vols. St. Paul: West Publishing, 1991.

Steers, Edward O., Jr. "Was Mistah Abe Babsized?" *Lincoln Herald* 101, no. 4 (Winter 1999): 164-170.

_____. *Blood on the Moon: The Assassination of Abraham Lincoln.* Lexington: University of Kentucky Press, 2001.

Stevens, Walter B. *A Reporter's Lincoln.* Lincoln: University of Nebraska Press, 1998.

Stoddard, William O. *Inside the White House in War Times: Memoirs and Reports of Lincoln's Secretary.* Lincoln: University of Nebraska Press, 2000.

Strozier, Charles B. *Lincoln's Quest for Union: Public and Private Meanings.* New York: Basic Books, 1982.

Tarbell, Ida M. *In the Footsteps of the Lincolns.* New York: Harper and Brothers, 1924.

Temple, Wayne C. *By Square and Compasses: The Building of the Lincoln Home and Its Saga.* Bloomington, Ill.: Ashler Press, 1984.

_____. *Abraham Lincoln: From Skeptic to Prophet.* Mahomet, Ill.: Mayhaven Publishing, 1995.

Theissen, Gerd, and Annette Merz. *The Historical Jesus: A Comprehensive Guide.* Translated by John Bowden. Minneapolis: Fortress Press, 1998.

Thomas, Benjamin P. *Portrait for Posterity: Lincoln and His Biographers.* New Brunswick, N.J.: Rutgers University Press, 1947.

_____. *Abraham Lincoln: A Biography.* New York: Modern Library, 1968.

_____. *Lincoln's New Salem.* Carbondale: Southern Illinois University Press, 1987.

Thurow, Glen E. "Abraham Lincoln's Political Religion." In *The Historian's Lincoln: Pseudohistory, Psychohistory, and History*, ed. Gabor S. Boritt, 125-143. Urbana: University of Illinois Press, 1996.

Trefousse, Hans L. *Andrew Johnson: A Biography*. New York: W. W. Norton, 1989.

Trueblood, David Elton. *Abraham Lincoln: Theologian of American Anguish*. New York: Harper & Row, 1973.

Turner, Justin G., and Linda Levitt Turner, eds. *Mary Todd Lincoln: Her Life and Letters*. New York: Knopf, 1972.

Van Voorst, Robert E. *Jesus Outside the New Testament: An Introduction to the Ancient Evidence*. Grand Rapids: William B. Eerdmans, 2000.

Von Bothmer, Bernard. "Devout Believer or Skeptic Politician? An Overview of Historians' Analyses of Abraham Lincoln's Religion: 1859-2001." *Lincoln Herald* 107, no. 4 (Winter 2005): 154-166.

Walsh, John Evangelist. *The Shadows Rise: Abraham Lincoln and the Ann Rutledge Legend*. Urbana: University of Illinois Press, 1993.

Warren, Louis A. *Lincoln's Parentage and Childhood: A History of the Kentucky Lincolns Supported by Documentary Evidence*. New York: Century, 1926.

_____. *Lincoln's Youth: The Indiana Years, Seven to Twenty-one, 1816-1830*. Indianapolis: Indiana Historical Society, 1991.

Weik, Jesse W. *The Real Lincoln: A Portrait*. Boston: Houghton Mifflin, 1922.

White, Ronald C., Jr. *Lincoln's Greatest Speech: The Second Inaugural*. New York: Simon & Schuster, 2002.

_____. *The Eloquent President: A Portrait of Lincoln Through His Words*. New York: Random House, 2005.

Wilson, Douglas L. *Lincoln Before Washington: New Perspectives on the Illinois Years*. Urbana: University of Illinois Press, 1997.

————. *Honor's Voice: The Transformation of Abraham Lincoln*. New York: Knopf, 1998.

————. *Lincoln's Sword: The Presidency and the Power of Words*. New York: Knopf, 2006.

Wilson, Douglas L., and Rodney O. Davis, eds. *Herndon's Informants: Letters, Interviews, and Statements About Abraham Lincoln*. Urbana: University of Illinois Press, 1998.

Winkle, Kenneth J. *The Young Eagle: The Rise of Abraham Lincoln*. Dallas: Taylor Trade Publishing, 2001.

Woldman, Albert A. *Lawyer Lincoln*. New York; Carroll & Graf, 1994.

Wolf, William J. *The Almost Chosen People: A Study of the Religion of Abraham Lincoln*. Garden City, N.Y.: Doubleday, 1959.

Wright, N. T. *What Saint Paul Really Said: Was Paul of Tarsus the Real Founder of Christianity?* Grand Rapids: William B. Eerdmans, 1997.

————. "The Divinity of Jesus." In Marcus J. Borg and N. T. Wright, *The Meaning of Jesus: Two Visions*, 157-168. San Francisco: HarperCollins, 1999.

Zall, P. M., ed. *Abe Lincoln Laughing: Humorous Anecdotes from Original Sources by and About Abraham Lincoln*. Knoxville: University of Tennessee Press, 1997.

Zarefsky, David. *Lincoln, Douglas, and Slavery: In the Crucible of Public Debate*. Chicago: University of Chicago Press, 1990.

Index

Acknowledgements

I would have never completed this book without the encouragement of Ed Steers. We were both speaking at a symposium on Lincoln in Chambersburg, Pennsylvania, and he convinced me to start writing a book that I had as an idea in my head for some time. Ed has always been encouraging, and he is a treasure in the Lincoln community. I have to also thank Frank McGraff for generously volunteering his time to help me make this book clearer.

This book would have not been possible without the hard work of Lincoln scholars who have made much of this wonderful primary source material available to the public. Douglas Wilson, Rodney Davis, Michael Burlingame, and Wayne Temple especially deserve credit for this. Special mention should also go to the brilliant contributions made in the area of Lincoln's religious and intellectual thought by Allen Guelzo. Of course any errors in fact or interpretation are my own.

My family has sustained me too in this process. My wife Beth was indulgent toward all my shortcomings during this process and was keen that I succeed. Sam, Maggie, and George have enriched my life and made this all worthwhile.

Others have helped me along the way with a question here or there. I must mention fellow teacher Roger Norton. His excellent Web site has introduced millions of students to Lincoln all over the world. My colleague Kim Gilmore has helped me too with suggestions and advice. Keya Morgan, who is preparing a book on Lincoln photographs, kindly gave me permission to reprint the picture of Eddie Lincoln.

Finally, I must thank Bruce H. Franklin and Noreen O'Connor-Abel of Westholme Publishing for believing in this project and making it work.